Stepping STONES

7 STEPS TO ACTIVATING YOUR DIVINE DESTINY

DR. JOELLE SUEL

Published by: Word Feed Press, LLC
13918 E. Mississipi Ave., #134
Aurora, CO 80012
303-357-1522
Author's Website: http://www.DrJoelle.org

Library of Congress Control Number: 2018912519

Edited by Rev. Linda Gawlik

Cover and interior design by Exodus Design
Christian Web & Graphic Design Studio

Printed in the U.S.A.

ISBN 978-0-9788700-1-0

TABLE OF CONTENTS

NOTE TO THE READER

God honors our hunger and I trust He will bless you above and beyond your expectations in the pursuit of the fulfillment of your destiny. He has placed this desire in your heart and will use this book as one of His many ways to guide you into what He has planned for you. We receive our calling as Ambassadors of Christ with gratitude and joyful expectation. I trust your journey will continue to be glorious and whatever you do will bear eternal fruit.

There are stepping stones that helped me, and they continue to guide me in accomplishing what the Lord leads me to do. You will understand them deeper and deeper at each level of growth *from glory to glory*, faith to faith, and strength to strength.

The seven-chapter titles build one by one in a specific order. That order is of great importance and speaks volumes. Each step interacts with the others. In the natural, the sequence of the chapters "Death", first, to "Divine Endowment", last, do not appear logical. It is what precedes "Divine Endowment" that makes its existence significant.

The order of these stepping stones is as important as the order in which we answer the call of God on our lives. Where do we start? Do we continue what we are doing? How do we go ahead? What does it take to serve the Most High God? In Luke 12:48 we read, "... For everyone to whom much is given, from him much will be required;" The wisdom keys communicated in each chapter will contribute to your growth and encourage you in the process.

After the titles come the key scriptures for the chapter about "counting." They each contain the same word: count. Count comes from the Greek word *logizomai,* meaning to reckon, to think on, or to consider. Each chapter covers a principle connected to this meaning. Meditating on these essential truths enables us to make firm decisions.

The Lord tells us in Luke 14:28, "For which of you, intending to build a tower, does not sit down first and count the cost, whether he has enough to finish it?" This book will help you achieve the directive of this scripture. The Lord will use these words to bring forth His will for your life. Each time you read it, the Holy Spirit will reveal more to you.

I have shared examples of my personal journey hoping it will strengthen yours. I suggest you complete the "reflection" and "action steps" given at the end of each chapter. These exercises will help you apply the contents and bring surety to your steps.

Prepare to walk in God's will while being encouraged by His love. His authority and anointing increases with each step you take. Put aside any preconceived ideas of the specifics of your call so you can receive fresh confirmation and revelation when needed. I trust He directed you to this study. What a stepping stone!

CHAPTER 1

Romans 6:8-11 *"Now if we died with Christ, we believe that we shall also live with Him, knowing that Christ, having been raised from the dead, dies no more. Death no longer has dominion over Him. For the death that He died, He died to sin once for all; but the life that He lives, He lives to God. Likewise you also, <u>reckon</u> yourselves to be dead indeed to sin, but alive to God in Christ Jesus our Lord."*

DEATH

THIS FIRST STEPPING STONE makes all the others succeed. It enables us to remain victorious and fulfill our divine destiny. The revelation of our identity in Christ lies within our willingness to die to everything that hinders us from the abundant life in Him.

Every believer in Jesus is called to experience transformation into His image, *from glory to glory*. It happens differently for each individual and it's only by God's grace that it occurs. We discover our new identity in Christ and seek His will for our divine destiny.

Our desire to obey the Lord faces numerous oppositions including our flesh. We are a spirit, we have a soul and live in a body. When we are born "again" (regeneration), our Spirit becomes alive. We are born anew from above and receive a new nature. The Spirit of God lives in us. Allowing Him to lead and direct us is "walking in the Spirit".

We are used to being controlled by our flesh. Flesh doesn't refer just to the physical part of us, but also to our soulish nature. The body is not evil in itself. In its negative usage, it relates to the ego, the "I" that is used to leading our decisions, but now must be subject to the Lord. That is the part we need to die to. As we die to our flesh, we liberate our spirit to obey the Lord.

> **Romans 6:11** "Likewise you also, reckon yourselves to be dead indeed to sin, but alive to God in Christ Jesus our Lord."

To reckon means to account for, to count something as done, to conclude an act, to complete. Chapter 6 of Romans emphasizes this truth and we must implement it to win the war with our flesh and walk in the Spirit as further explained in chapters 7 and 8 of Romans. We cannot count ourselves as being alive to God through our Lord Jesus Christ without first counting ourselves as being dead to sin. Symbolically, we were crucified with the Lord. Therefore, in the same manner, we identify with His resurrection.

 There cannot be a resurrection if there is no crucifixion.

When we travel abroad, we show our identification to enter another country.

 Our identification in Christ gives us access to new realms of the reality of His glory.

We enter areas of new freedoms and attain great peace. Our identity in Christ is the reality we walk in daily. It takes place in our hearts.

War

We discover challenges as we proceed to walk in the newness of life we received in Christ. We do what we don't want to do, and not what we want to do. Our hearts long to study the Word of God; however, our flesh watches tv. Our spirit calls us to pray while our flesh calls us to sleep. It is the excess in anything our flesh wants or demands that we need to overcome. Anything unhealthy and out of balance can bind us and make us unable to make healthy choices.

> **Romans 7:18-19** "I know that in me (that is, in my flesh) nothing good dwells; for to will is present with me, but *how* to perform what is good I do not find. For the good that I will *to do,* I do not do; but the evil I will not *to do,* that I practice."

For some, it is an addiction that we battle. This war between our Spirit and our flesh rages on and we plunge into despair when we are unable to conquer it.

 Trying so hard to do so in our own strength often binds us even more because we focus on the problem more than the solution.

We experience turmoil when we cannot stop doing what we no longer desire to do! What is the answer to this conflict?

Galatians 5:16-17 "I say then: Walk in the Spirit, and you shall not fulfill the lust of the flesh. For the flesh lusts against the Spirit, and the Spirit against the flesh; and these are contrary to one another so that you do not do the things that you wish."

Our relationship with the Lord establishes our walk with Him. Without fellowship there cannot be a partnership. When anything tries to rise from our old man, we must regard it as destroyed. It is not destroyed to the point of nonexistence but rendered inactive and powerless. Then we can be free from temptation, even when it is all around us, because we now live by faith and learn to yield to the presence of the Holy Spirit in our lives.

Death to the flesh is a very important milestone in our walk. The timing differs for every one of us. When it occurs, we never forget because it moves us into another realm of experiencing the reality of the life of Christ in us. The Spirit of Christ leads us to that place of death to the flesh as He reveals the reality of all that He accomplished on the cross. This reality becomes alive to us when we identify with Jesus in His death and resurrection.

 The cross represents the crossroad where the flesh and the spirit intersect.

It makes a vital separation between the two.

I remember one of my encounters...

I rushed outside into the piercing cold and shivered. My hands gripped my coat and pulled it tighter around me for more warmth. As I squinted my eyes, I pulled a cigarette out of my pocket. My shaking hands struggled to place the cigarette between my freezing lips. Lighting it challenged my coordination and the unsteady flame nearly singed my hair. As I deeply inhaled the first puff, it suddenly dawned on me that this was a stupid act on my part. Here I was outside, in the winter, to smoke a Kool light! What bondage! If this addiction to cigarettes led me to stand on a porch on a freezing snowy day, there was no end to its overpowering control. The Holy Spirit convicted me, and I observed myself as though I was outside my body looking at me. *This doesn't portray who I am as a child of God*, I thought. *How can I stop? This addiction is killing me!* The enemy's voice pounded my soul, "You can't give it up. You can't conquer this weakness. Impossible!" I stabbed the cigarette into the snow to put it out and ran inside sobbing. *Please, Lord, set me free!*

I sought the Lord daily for freedom. The moment I received Jesus in my heart, some fleshy desires ceased while this addiction to smoking remained. In error, I assumed that drinking, drugs and intimacy with my boyfriend would be harder to conquer. It wasn't. For three years, every method I tried to beat the addiction to nicotine failed. This constant failure increased both my anxiety and my despair.

I would search the scriptures on bondage, the flesh, discipline and any other topic I could think of that might shed light on my inability to conquer smoking. While looking for answers, I still inhaled the smoke. I struggled with an unshakable sense of inadequacy, guilt and self-condemnation. In prayer, the Lord kept reminding me of His love and how I belonged to Him. He was always drawing me closer to Him. Thank you, Lord!

I remember when this spiritual warfare ended. On that day, in the Bible reading the "reckon" in Romans 6:11 became so clear. The verse jumped off the page. It revealed my position in Christ and I wept from all it implied. I understood how baptism illustrated my identification with the Lord's death, burial and resurrection.

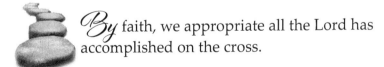 *By* faith, we appropriate all the Lord has accomplished on the cross.

After work on that Friday, March 17, my heart was leaping with joy, *Lord, thank you for my freedom.* This was the day I planned for my "burial". When I was water baptized before, I did not fully understand its significance. Its symbolism of the burial of the old man, my flesh, was unknown to me. After I unhooked the phone and locked the door, I proceeded with this ceremonial rite with a sense of excitement. While the bathtub filled with warm water, I lit a candle, opened the Bible to Romans 6 and turned on soft instrumental worship music.

When I first stepped into the water, I stood while I read the chapter and then I noticed the pack of cigarettes laying next to the sink. I got out of the water and with determination flushed all the cigarettes down the toilet. Right away, the enemy tried to attack me with fear and hopelessness. "You should have kept one in case this doesn't work." I rebuked him at once, stepped back into the water and sat down. The Lord revealed to me that I needed to submerge my whole body; I couldn't do this one part at a time.

This symbolic burial must be a total immersion. In the natural, we do not bury one part of the body at a time. We bury the whole body. Water baptism is a perfect application of this principle. We submerge our whole body into the water. In doing so, we identify with the death of our Lord on the cross and consider our fleshy tendencies now dead. We identify with His resurrection as we rise out of the water in newness of life.

> **Romans 6:4-5** "Therefore we were buried with Him through baptism into death, that just as Christ was raised from the dead by the glory of the Father, even so we also should walk in newness of life. For if we have been united together in the likeness of His death, certainly we also shall be in the likeness of His resurrection."

 We conquer the power of our weaknesses, empowered by the Spirit of Christ.

It's a moment by moment victory. When we fail, we receive God's love and grace. We rest in Him knowing His strength is perfected in our weaknesses. What freedom we have when at last we walk in newness of life, His resurrection power, *from glory to glory!*

The burial needed to be complete...

Jesus, I confess you as my Lord and Savior! I believe you died for my sins, were buried and rose on the third day. I'm a new creation in you and as an act of my faith, I now identify with your crucifixion as I go into the water; and your resurrection as I come out. I felt the Lord was with me in the bath dunking me. His small voice whispering, *I want all of you. Leave your battles behind you in the water. I love you. I am with you.* At once I immersed my whole body in the water.

I pictured the person I used to be before being born again, the old man dead, including the desire for cigarettes. Then getting out of the water seeing the new person, the new me, rise. After years of trying to quit smoking, I was free. There were no withdrawal symptoms from the nicotine. For a short time, the enemy still sought to entice me with cigarettes, but to no avail.

I realize the Lord could have removed the addiction just as He had removed other things, but then I wouldn't have sought Him like I did. I would have thought I was the one who was strong enough to quit. God is more interested in our fellowship with Him, so we can grow into the knowledge of who He is and pursue what He has for us.

How could I answer His call if I answered my flesh above His will for my life?

Baptism is an outward expression of what we believe in our hearts. For many, remembering what their baptism represents helps them apply its meaning. Day by day we identify with the Lord, by faith, so we can walk in victory.

From that dying moment on, I followed the Holy Spirit with more confidence in His leading. It was a turning point in my life. Death to flesh changed my outlook on everything around me. Selfishness and self-centeredness started to fade away and Christ-centeredness increased. It was no longer about me, but about Him. Day by day I yielded to His blessed touch and learned to flow with His waves of glory. I continue to seek His divine ability to walk with Him. The more I learn, the more I realize I have much more to comprehend. Only by His grace can we grow, *from glory to glory.*

We *reckon* we have been crucified with Christ already, but must die daily to appropriate this great truth. We do so through partaking communion, reflecting on all that was accomplished on the cross. There will always be things we battle. After this initial dying to the flesh, dying daily becomes a moment by moment decision and a lesson on how to let go as we trust God and reach for His will. Returning to the foot of the cross through meditation and communion are ways to reckon ourselves dead and ways to appreciate what a wonderful gift God has given us through His ultimate sacrifice.

Trust

To trust is to have confidence in; to have an assured reliance on the character, ability, strength or truth of someone or something. We attain it as we grow in the knowledge of that someone or something.

 To trust God for what He can do, we must meditate on who He is and as we grasp His character, we rely on His ability. It's to the same degree we know the Lord that we can trust Him.

We believe He is the same yesterday, today and forever. He has delivered us from spiritual death. The one who raises the dead can deliver us out of any trying circumstances. Our God loves us! His goodness and faithfulness amaze us, and His glory is more than enough! As we trust, we learn to surrender.

> **2 Corinthians 1:9-10** "Yes, we had the sentence of death in ourselves, that we should not trust in ourselves but in God who raises the dead, who delivered us from so great a death, and does deliver us; in whom we trust that He will still deliver *us*."

After we surrender ourselves to the Lord, our willingness to surrender things dear to us is tested. To surrender means to yield or give up one's self or turn over into the hands of another. We can surrender all to the Lord as our trust in Him grows from faith to faith.

God often leads us to relinquish anything that has more power over us than it should. To have to give up harmful things is obvious. It's more of a challenge to submit back to Him the blessings He places in our hands: our mate, children, vocation, or ministry.

 To answer the call of God, we need to turn over to Him that divine call, so He can accomplish it in and through us without our flesh getting in the way.

If we don't, the call on our lives could become more important to us than our relationship with Him. As we seek His will, it's best not to limit ourselves to a specific function.

Abraham offered up Isaac, the son He loved, in obedience to God. He walked in the faith we walk in many times in our lives: *"the faith that relies on God in all situations."* Abraham counted on the power of God to raise Isaac. Not only did he know God *could* do it, he also had faith He *would* do it.

In our hearts, we continue surrendering all things to God, and as we do, we find we can walk free from bondages. We leave in His hands what He places in ours, trusting He holds *us* in His.

The trust in ourselves decreases as our trust in God increases.

 When Christ becomes our motive for ministry, doors open for Him, not for us.

All must be done for His glory and His alone. The Apostle Paul was determined to see the glory of Christ manifested through him to further the gospel and the honor of His name. We should also have the same desire. However, it is not something we do ourselves. It comes from the Holy Spirit.

In the natural, if we get arrested, we surrender to the authorities and lift both hands. Spiritually, when we surrender to the Lord, we release what's in our hands, so we can lift them up to Him. We can't hold on to our worries and give them to the Lord at the same time. We cast our cares upon Him with confidence in His divine ability. We might have to do it more than once! It becomes easier when we witness His divine interventions.

After we give up what the Holy Spirit asks, we remind ourselves we cannot return to the Lord and ask Him to give it back to us. We learn, *from glory to glory*, to trust Him even when we see no immediate changes. Our surrender opens the way to deep healing. Oh, to launch into the depths of complete surrender!

After I quit smoking, dying daily came through constant tests of trust. As a single mother of two girls, I struggled to make ends meet and worried about their whereabouts and the challenges we faced. When the rent was short, dying to my flesh meant, *I'm scared Lord. I don't know how I can pay it, but I die to what I feel and think and surrender to your care in total trust.* It wasn't easy, and many times, tears and fears arose. When the provisions came, my trust in Him grew. With each step of faith, I turned to Him and discovered He provides in unexpected ways.

Let Go

The accomplishments we desire to achieve requires that we let go of everything that might hinder our progress. Jumping out of an airplane is a helpful illustration of this process.

The plane represents our places of dependency, things we know so well, our comfort zone. It is anything that God leads us to move *out* of to move *in Him*, in a greater way. It includes our past failures and successes, familiarity, circumstances, and anything else that represents our own life lived for us alone. Oh yes, we can relate to Paul in the previous scripture of 2 Corinthians 1:9-10 and truly say, *"He gave himself for me. Now surely, I can give my life to Him and trust Him with it because it is His!"*

It is easier to stay in the plane than to jump out into the unknown even if we fear it will crash. Although God has many parachutes prepared for us, He will open them only when needed. The ripcord to release them is in His hands. Parachutes are all the things He brings to prevent us from falling. They are the ways of escape He makes when we see the ground and the supernatural release of provision, protection and guidance when worry blurs our vision. His parachute is the helping hand, the second wind, the last-minute answer, and His glory manifested from faith to faith.

We are not to question or fear that He might not open our parachute in time. God activates His sovereignty outside the comfort zone (airplane) of our own life.

 Our desire to obey Him outweighs our fears.

Trusting the parachute to open when necessary is the best way I can describe the step of faith God asks of all his servants. When we jump and take that step of faith, we can trust the *parachute* He opens contains His love, His faith, His touch, His joy, His peace, His omnipotence… *Him!* God leads us out of the airplanes, so we can learn to trust and experience Him.

After we take that one step of faith and jump out the first time, it becomes easier. We look forward to the exhilaration of doing it again and again as we encounter God's supernatural ways. To be out of the plane is to walk in the spirit.

Situations might cause us to return to the plane. We do so unaware. It happens when the people we care about are in dire situations. Our mind thinks the only way to help them is to go where they are, but our spirit knows we should remain outside trusting in the Lord. We help them from where we are, and they will jump out and trust Him when they are ready.

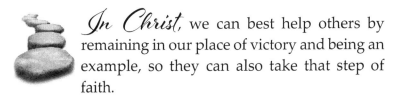 *In Christ,* we can best help others by remaining in our place of victory and being an example, so they can also take that step of faith.

We may also go back into the plane because we look at the problem instead of the answer as fear grips us. When we set our mind on earthly things instead of seeking those things above, fear tells us that the parachute might not deploy. In addition, we long to be part of the familiar. People, situations, and habits we are accustomed to draw us back. When we find ourselves on that plane again, we must put our focus back on the spiritual realm. Oh, to live in the realm of His glory!

Philippians 1:21 "For to me, to live is Christ, and to die is gain."

Our conceptual planes vary but the principle remains the same. With every new spiritual height, our planes move higher and higher requiring even a greater jump of faith.

I recall one of those times. I refer to it whenever I face a new airplane or the same plane at a new level...

My eyes opened wide with excitement. *Today the radio show starts. Hallelujah!* As I jumped out of bed, I felt a sharp pain and a throbbing throughout my mouth. *What's happening?* I rushed into the bathroom to look in a mirror. The sight of many canker sores on my gums added fear to the excruciating pain. I gargled with warm saltwater and prayed, *Lord, you called me to share your Word on the radio, remove these sores so I can do so, I pray. I take authority over these symptoms and command them to go, in Jesus Name.* My shower, protein shake and getting dressed unfolded in an automated fashion. My thoughts couldn't stop at the situation in this plane of despair. Even if the sores remained, I purposed to obey the Lord and trust His parachute of supernatural ability. God often instructs us when the situation in the natural appears impossible. We keep our eyes on Him and hold on!

The recording area in the radio station contained two tables facing each other. The presenter guided me to one side, positioned the microphone in front of my mouth and handed me headphones. "I will run a sound check," he explained as he walked out. Here it was, time to fly! If I focused on the sores just one split second, I would go back to the plane and defeat would be evident. "Ready? " I heard. *Lord, take over, I pray* came forth. "1, 2, 3, go!" the presenter instructed. The anointing of the Lord came upon me and for 15 minutes I disappeared. He took over and His words ministered to the listeners. Thank you, Lord. Hallelujah!

This jump made a way for many others, and with each one what mattered was being sure He was the one leading, not me. Each time, the scenario differs. God doesn't want us to limit the ways He moves. There is a constant thread in spiritual warfare. The enemy attacks us most right before we step out, and right after.

 When you know you have died to the flesh, and live in the spirit in Christ, you can tell satan, *"you can't kill me, I'm already dead."*

Death to our flesh, just like a natural death, should not be feared. Our Lord took the sting out of death, and through the cross we have eternal life.

1 Corinthians 15:55-58 "O DEATH, WHERE IS YOUR STING? O HADES, WHERE IS YOUR VICTORY? The sting of death is sin, and the strength of sin is the law. But thanks be to God, who gives us the victory through our Lord Jesus Christ. Therefore, my beloved brethren, be steadfast, immovable, always abounding in the work of the Lord, knowing that your labor is not in vain in the Lord."

The glory of death is the power of the resurrection manifested fully in and through us by the Holy Spirit.

Since that experience I find our planes go to different heights to teach us to apply this principle of dependence from faith to faith. We learn the way to walk in faith remains the same: complete surrender to His caring hands.

In conclusion regarding this first stepping stone, we know we have died to ourselves when it is no longer our will, but His will that we want accomplished. At the place where we come to the end of ourselves, He *then* begins. When we will do whatever it takes to obey Him, regardless of the cost, He *then* steps in. As we give up, He *then* takes us up to another level of trust.

After we have tried things our own way and are ready to allow Him to have His way, He *then* leads the way.

How glorious to die daily so He can live!

Moment by moment we learn, and will continue to learn, how to decrease so He may increase. Our obedience makes way to more than we know. Expect clarity to unfold as you follow His leading through each chapter. Your launching has begun!

Reflection

- How do you handle the war between the flesh and the spirit?

- What strongholds have you conquered through Christ, and what is He working on?

- How did you recognize you had "died" to the flesh?

- How have you experienced being "buried"?

- Recall an example of a time you stepped out of a plane and then jumped back in. What hindered you and what did you learn?

Action Steps

1 Make a list of the planes the Lord is showing you to jump out of and trust Him.

2 Pray and decide a date for each jump.

3 Note the parachutes you trust God to deploy.

Prayer

Father, I say yes!

Help me be the person You called me to be, and to do what You called me to do. I count my flesh crucified and I am alive in You. Enable me to obey Your leading as I surrender and let go of whatever tries to hold me back. I trust Your parachutes will open for me whenever You lead me to jump out of some situations. Help me cast my cares upon You and trust You with my life and the lives of my loved ones. I look to You. Thank You for anointing each step I take so that it may glorify You. I love You and surrender all, in Jesus' name.

Amen.

CHAPTER 2

Luke 14:28-33 *"For which of you, intending to build a tower, does not sit down first, and count the cost, whether he has enough to finish it—lest after he has laid the foundation, and is not able to finish, all who see it begin to mock him, saying, This man began to build and was not able to finish. Or what king, going to make war against another king, does not sit down first, and consider whether he is able with ten thousand to meet him who comes against him with twenty thousand? Or else, while the other is still a great way off, he sends a delegation and asks conditions of peace. So likewise, whosoever of you does not forsake all that he has cannot be My disciple."*

DISCIPLESHIP

We cannot take this SECOND STEPPING STONE OF DISCIPLESHIP in answering the call of God with surety if we do not die daily to the flesh. That first stepping stone, death, continuously helps us with all the others, especially discipleship. Discipleship is significant in our divine calling and we must seek it regardless of what we are called to do.

Forsake All?

To be a disciple, we are to forsake all.

> **Luke 14:33** "So likewise, whoever of you does not forsake all that he has cannot be My disciple."

What are we to relinquish? To accurately count the cost, it is necessary to recognize what we own and where we are now.

 We cannot ascertain how to reach a future position without first assessing our current one.

A step might be missed in the process and hinder what we are to possess. Truth in our assessment of what is now will help us speed up the process of where we are going.

MapQuest cannot give us directions to an address without knowing our departing point. We should not only evaluate our current situation but also the situations of those to whom we minister. I often found in ministering that I might think people were in a certain place and I tried to direct them to where they needed to go, but the place where they were right then, was not where I thought. When we meet people who speak little, it's easy to put words in their mouths and assume we know their position. These assumptions can bring misunderstandings and hinder the help we bring. As we learn to lean on Christ, we seek Him for each individual because our own natural knowledge is limited. It's a personal walk indeed. Praise the Lord for His faithfulness! He knows everyone's starting point and teaches accordingly.

If your child starts kindergarten and on the first day asks, "Which way should I go," would you tell your little kindergartner, "Find your own way?" No, you would lead and continue to guide. You would do so when your child goes to middle school, high school, college and at every needed turn. Our Heavenly Father delights in leading us when we ask Him.

For every purchase, there is a determined price. Before buying an item, one must consider its value. As Christians, we have been bought with a precious price: the blood of our Lord Jesus Christ that was shed on the cross. He valued us so much that He sacrificed His life for us. He purchased our salvation through the cross and we now have free access to it by faith. The cost of discipleship is another matter. Christ died for us to give us life. Now we must die for Him, so He can live through us.

 We must forsake all for the sake of the call.

It is when we can no longer count on ourselves that we can count on His grace, faithfulness, strength, ability and power. He will make a way when there seems to be no way. We start from point zero and die to gain all of Him and none of ourselves. The life that we live is by faith.

> **Galatians 2:20** "I have been crucified with Christ; it is no longer I who live; but Christ lives in me; and the life which I now live in the flesh I live by faith in the Son of God, who loved me and gave himself for me."

It costs us everything to follow Him. When we start at zero, we need not have any fear of losing anything.

 When we, and all we have belong to the Lord, we do not have to worry about how to keep it.

He shows us what we can depend on and that leads us to count on Him alone. He is our Rock, and all else is sinking sand.

God uses both the known and unknown training we have gained in our past. He gives us wisdom for our decisions. We cannot count on everything that comes from us, or others, and move forward without counting on Him above all: it is *His* ability, *His* presence, and *His* leading in *His* ways. He accomplishes His will in His perfect timing and according to His process. We cannot be a disciple if we don't follow Him. We assess what we own, then the Lord leads us not to depend on our own resources, but to use them in obedience to His will, for His glory, and in His timing.

When on a mission trip to Africa I packed a little nightlight, a net for protection against the mosquitoes and cream to guard against bugs. I carried all of my "just in case" items like Advil in case of a headache, Aloe Vera for sunburn and Neosporin for an infection. I included my CD player, CDs, earphones and a few books. I even thought of bringing the cleaner you can use without water, my mints and a special bath sponge.

After ministering at a revival in London, I was scheduled for another one in Cameroon, Africa, so I planned to travel there directly. At two in the morning they rushed me to the airport, so I wouldn't miss my flight. I checked my luggage and carried my purse onto the plane. When arriving in Africa, I waited for two hours before discovering they had lost my suitcase. I proceeded to the Delta airlines counter. They said, "We apologize. It could take one to two weeks before your luggage is located. Here are four clothing vouchers of $20.00 each to help buy a few clothes."

The host pastor drove me to my quarters: a twin bed with no pillow, a sheet, a 24-inch side table and a few crawling insects. All the things I had packed would have come in handy. I knelt and prayed, *Father I don't have any of the things I prepared but I have what matters the most, You. Help me obey your will, with grace, by your spirit.* My phone service didn't reach the United States so communication with my loved ones was impossible. I'm so grateful for the prayers that reach above and beyond the natural! They recovered my items ten days later. By then I had gained what no material things could have ever given me: more dependence on the Lord, the ability to stand and war, and an unshakable knowledge of His abiding presence. To this day He continues to teach me these lessons anew. Thank you, Lord!

We can expect opposition and perils. When events surprise us, fear comes.

To expect the unexpected helps us grow in awareness and not be moved.

When we build our house upon a rock, the floods come, the winds blow and beat upon it, but it cannot fall because the foundation is sure. There is no foundation that can be laid other than Jesus Christ, the Chief Cornerstone.

> **Matthew 7:24-25** "Therefore whoever hears these sayings of Mine, and does them, I will liken him to a wise man who built his house on the rock: and the rain descended, the floods came, and the winds blew and beat on that house; and it did not fall, for it was founded on the rock."

It is easier to build when our only sure foundation is Him, having already given our all to Him. We can then forsake all for His sake. It is also important not to give up as we wait for victory.

It's one thing to start a race; another to finish it. We need to sit down and count the cost as we walk by faith, moment by moment. This does not imply procrastination in answering the call but a desire for wisdom.

 *Never* stop
starting.

We keep pursuing our goals even when we fail. Mistakes do not cause us to stop. We start again, and again. We are to keep on keeping on regardless of any unforeseen circumstances we may encounter and as overcomers we continue to yield to His leading.

Learn Christ

Becoming and making disciples is the primary mandate of this Great Commission given to us by our Lord, Jesus Christ.

> **Matthew 28:19-20** "Go therefore and make disciples of all the nations, baptizing them in the name of the Father and of the Son and of the Holy Spirit, teaching them to observe all things that I have commanded you; and lo, I am with you always, even to the end of the age." Amen."

The Greek word for disciple is *mathetes*, which comes from the word *matheo*, meaning to learn, or *mathano*, meaning a learner, or pupil. There is an active element in this meaning. It is an action word. Hence, the sense is more than just head knowledge. It implies doing and putting into practice.

Our subject is Jesus Christ. We don't just know about Him, we learn the reality of who He is. As we are transformed into His image, we learn to understand how He moves and how He handles situations.

As we seek a heart knowledge, we learn to go through things in life because of *who* we know, not *what* we know.

The people around us see He is alive as they watch our lives. They see His joy and His peace manifested through us daily whether at home, at work, at a baseball game, at a social gathering, and even through trials and hard times. The experiential knowledge we walk in demonstrates our growth in knowing Him.

The Holy Spirit teaches us who Christ is, what He would do and how He thinks. We find He gives us lessons through unbelievers, movies, books and any other way He so desires. Each one of us hears different things out of the same sermon because He teaches us what we need. We can expect to receive from Him in every situation. While we learn directly from Him, He also teaches us through others by example or wise counsel. He answers our requests for divine wisdom in seemingly impossible situations.

As we disciple others, we discover that He teaches them through us, whether we notice it or not. Teaching is more than giving instructions, it's leading through actions.

 What we do portrays a greater message than what we say.

Some are willing and desire to be taught because of the example we give. It is only to the extent that we are a disciple that we can teach others to be disciples and to disciple others.

When we see others walking with the Lord, it encourages and strengthens our own growth and increases our faith. What we do shares a much greater message than our words. We conclude the Word is true because it works, and its fruit is evident. It is difficult to believe a person if they say one thing and do another. It diminishes our trust in their integrity. We are ambassadors of Christ and represent Him everywhere we go. We still fail from time to time, and *from glory to glory*, but we continue to yield to Him for our continued growth as disciples. We are often unaware of others watching our walk as we are led by the Holy Spirit and lead others by example.

> **John 8:31-32** "Then Jesus said to those Jews who believed Him, 'If you abide in My word, you are My disciples indeed. And you shall know the truth, and the truth shall make you free.'"

The Lord teaches us His Word as we walk in the truth of it. The truth we learn sets us free to the point that we can walk in it and the Word may manifest Himself through us. We hear the Word, but in declaring and doing it, the truth it carries renews our mind.

The Lord is our Master. He leads: we follow. We do not go our own way and ask Him to follow us. Our willingness to be taught the newness of life in which we are to walk requires us to deny ourselves, our familiar steps, and our former conduct.

In other words, we must say no to the former to say yes to the new.

Ephesians 4:20-24 "But you have not so learned Christ, if indeed you have heard Him and have been taught by Him, as the truth is in Jesus: That you put off, concerning your former conduct, the old man which grows corrupt according to the deceitful lusts, and be renewed in the spirit of your mind, and that you put on the new man which was created according to God in true righteousness and holiness."

It is when we "put off" that we "put on". The new man, created in righteousness and true holiness, cannot live apart from the vine to which it belongs. As we abide in Him, and His words abides in us, we bear much fruit. He is glorified, and we are His disciples indeed.

The Lord desires for us to be fruitful and multiply. We minister His life to one another. For example, if we have just learned a lesson on patience we are able to be patient with others. As we do so, we share His life and demonstrate His character. The more we abide in Him, the more intimate with Him we become. We are then quicker to recognize Him in our circumstances. He shows us how to walk in His grace and handle difficult situations with divine wisdom.

Our ministry is always to the Lord first. Only then are we able to minister to others. This entails a constant awareness of His presence. We acknowledge Him in everything we do. We worship Him, fellowship with Him, seek His will, His ways and His Word above all. We minister to others as a representative of Him, and we put others above ourselves. Always remember, when we meet a friend for lunch, attend a family gathering or interact with co-workers, we bring with us the Word of Life.

As disciples, we ask the Lord how He wants us to minister. It can never be to show "what" we know, but "who".

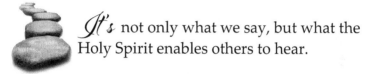 *It's* not only what we say, but what the Holy Spirit enables others to hear.

It's from the heart, not the head. We prepare to obey His leading at any moment. The Holy Spirit fills our mouths when needed. It's not up to us to determine what others comprehend. It is the Holy Spirit who teaches. We serve as His instruments and give Him all the glory!

In praying for others, we yield to what He has for that person and we do not try to comprehend it. When others ask us to pray for a specific situation, we take heed to them, give them our full attention, compassion and understanding and we pray for God's will, ways and truth for them. Otherwise, we could inadvertently agree with a lie if what is told to us is not the truth. There are some things the Lord will show us that are not for us to share. The Word of Knowledge may be for another time. As a disciple, we are led by the Spirit for discernment.

The Lord doesn't always lead us to help someone. He may have answers coming through other individuals. We pray and trust the Holy Spirit to continue to minister to others in a situation even after we have left their presence. The spiritual realm is greater than what we can see. We can rest in Him for His intended results!

Bear Your Cross

To bear our cross is to deny ourselves and acknowledge Him. Before we are born again, what we think of as life is not complete or whole. Operating in the flesh, the world system, our being alive is determined by others and the result is often tragic. Our lives then fluctuate up or down based on our expectations and only bring an appearance of fulfillment. We learn by the Spirit that others are no longer responsible for our happiness.

 *When* we start walking in newness of life, we realize what was can no longer *be*.

Our life is in the spirit, not in the flesh.

As we recognize that Christ has become our life, we grow from the place of Him being *a part* of our life, to Him *being our life*. Then His life becomes what connects us to others, and He flows through all our relationships bringing true contentment. Every relationship we have must be of a lesser priority than our relationship with Him. This does not mean that we don't care about others.

His love can flow more freely in and through us to others when they can no longer dictate our oneness with Him.

Luke 14:26-27 "If anyone comes to Me and does not hate his father and mother, wife and children, brothers and sisters, yes, and his own life also, he cannot be my disciple. And whosoever doth not bear his cross, and come after me, cannot be my disciple."

The word hate in this scripture means to love less. We love the Lord more than anyone or anything. Then the verse says to bear our cross and follow Him. We do so when we remember that the things trying to hold us back were nailed on the cross. We pick up what He provided in exchange through the cross. For example, we nail rejection to the cross and receive the acceptance He provided. We nail sickness and receive healing. We nail fear and receive love.

To follow Him, we guard against following others.

We cannot seek God's approval and man's approval at the same time.

Some people will not understand our new behaviors and will try to get us to return to our old destructive behaviors and habits. It's important to die to the need of another's approval. We learn to be influenced by the Lord's acceptance above all. Our goal should be to please God, not mankind.

When we are free from the need for people's acceptance and approval, it causes a breakthrough of holy boldness in our lives. I call it the "Teflon Anointing." Teflon describes the pots and pans that are nonstick. Offenses as well as compliments must drop off. If they "stick," they, instead of the Holy Spirit, will start leading us. We must shake off hindrances continuously until they no longer stick.

 We cannot expect from others what only God can give.

The spirit of rejection opposes our calling and we must put it under subjection as soon as it surfaces. This lie says that we are not worthy, but the truth is the Lord counts us as valuable. So much so that He willingly died for us. The lie shouts that no one is interested in us, that we will not be accepted, and we shouldn't pursue God's purpose. It shows up most when we are growing as a disciple. When we don't heed that false spirit, we show others the abundant life of Christ that we carry for His glory. We are the elect of God. Hallelujah!

When God led me to minister to others through a radio program, my natural mind questioned the idea. I was rejecting myself when I tried to make sense of it. *What about my French accent? I have no experience. I cannot afford it.* There was no way I thought I would be able to complete this assignment.

For four months, I did nothing about it even though it kept coming up in my spirit.

At that time, I worked in the accounting department of a foster care agency. There I met a Pastor who worked as a counselor and had had a radio program for many years. I shared with him that I was led to start a radio program and asked how that could be possible. He replied, "Here is the phone number of the director of the radio station. Meet him and see what the Lord does."

I remember sitting in the office of the manager of the radio station, my heart pounding, rebuking the fear of rejection. He said, "What would you like to start with, a fifteen or a thirty-minute program? Once or three times a week?" My thoughts raced. *You mean the answer is yes? This is happening? I can't afford five minutes.* To my surprise, I answered: "Let's start with 3 times a week." I signed the contract and walked back to my car as though I was on a cloud; my heart filled with praises and gratitude. The Lord led the director to take a huge step of faith by allowing me to host my program, "Glory to Glory," and I'm grateful for his obedience to the leading of the Lord to this day. I praise God for the awesome divine connections He places in our paths. We can count on Him to direct us to what is needed to go forth in His calling. When I received the first bill, I almost looked at it but sensed the Lord say: *my will, my bill.* That program expanded to five days a week and lasted eight years. Our faith cannot be based on the number of zeros after a number. I learned to never focus on costs when obeying His will.

Someone said, "when He decides — He provides," and that is so true. The challenge is to perceive without a shadow of a doubt that something is His will. When we die to self and walk in discipleship, we learn to heed and obey one step at a time. We may fall, trip and take a few wrong turns, but we keep going and growing with a willing heart. We discard the opinion of others when it hinders our obedience to God. Hearing God continues to be part of our daily walk.

We must become, and remain, teachable.

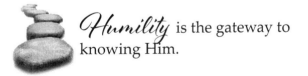

Humility is the gateway to knowing Him.

Discipleship never ends. How can we learn if we are no longer teachable? If we think we already know what a scripture says, we close our ears to fresh revelation. The Word of God is alive! Some of the greatest messages I have heard were taught from very familiar verses. One of my personal daily prayers has always been to remain teachable. In doing so, I realize how much I do not know and I want to learn more. His Word is new every morning. He continues to give me fresh revelation each day. When I think I really know a scripture, He gently shows me there is so much more! The Word that abides in me continues to grow as I let Him reveal more of His mysteries. Selah!

As we humble ourselves, He gives us grace and divine ability. We discover more of Him as we draw nigh to Him and He draws nigh to us. When conflicts arise with others, we seek a resolution, reconciliation and restoration. The response we receive may be the opposite of what we were seeking. What matters is that we pursue it and leave the results in God's hands.

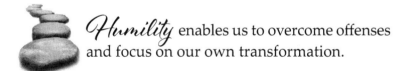

Humility enables us to overcome offenses and focus on our own transformation.

In conclusion, regarding this important step in answering His call, we learn as disciples that as we abide in Him, we ask what we will, and it shall be done unto us as it is written in John 15:7–8. "If you abide in Me, and My words abide in you, you will ask what you desire, and it shall be done for you. By this My Father is glorified, that you bear much fruit; so you will be My disciples." What a promise!

Reflection

- Recall when you were not able to count on yourself and found that you could count on God's grace to pull you through. How did this help strengthen your faith?

- How would you explain "bearing your cross"?

- How do you apply "never stop starting" to your life?

- How do you handle rejection?

- How has being teachable helped you? What helps you remain teachable?

Action Steps

1 Make a list of things you want to nail to the cross, and what you want to receive in its place.

2 Assess what you have now. What further "cost" do you see as necessary for what the Lord is leading you to do?

3 How could you improve your relationship with those you disciple through your actions?

Prayer

Father,

Thank You for teaching me who You are, Your Word, Your will and Your ways. Please help me remain humble and teachable. Deliver me from rejection, pride and unforgiveness. I pray, by Your grace, that my actions will show my discipleship and that I will be able to make disciples of others. Oh, that I may walk and talk in public as I do in private. Lord, You have called me to be an Ambassador for You and I gratefully accept. I love You! in Jesus' name.

Amen.

CHAPTER 3

Philippians 3:7-8 *"But what things were gain to me, these I have counted loss for Christ. Yet indeed I also count all things loss for the excellence of the knowledge of Christ Jesus my Lord, for whom I have suffered the loss of all things, and count them as rubbish, that I may gain Christ."*

DEDICATION

THE THIRD STEPPING STONE, dedication, enables our devotion and commitment to the Lord to be consistent and strengthens our foundation.

 The more we are set apart for Him, the more God shows us what He has set apart for us.

Will

To be dedicated to Christ requires total consecration. We consecrate a person or place to Him to be available for His use as He wills. We do so as we surrender our will to His, *from glory to glory.*

> **Romans 12:1-2** "I beseech you therefore, brethren, by the mercies of God, that you present your bodies a living sacrifice, holy, acceptable to God, *which* is your reasonable service. And do not be conformed to this world, but be transformed by the renewing of your mind, that you may prove what is that good and acceptable and perfect will of God."

Whatever Paul thought was personal gain prior to his conversion was afterward counted loss for Christ. He was completely dedicated to Christ.

 *Anything* that hinders us from the excellency of the knowledge of Christ is worth losing.

Paul clearly *counts* as rubbish the knowledge, experience, and understanding he acquired prior to his born again experience. In doing so, his knowledge of Christ increased and was released. God uses the things of our past for His glory. He has a way of bringing to nothing all things of our past so that He can be our everything. Then God uses those things to testify to others. Thus, He uses what we have gained when we are no longer dependent on that knowledge to serve Him. Gaining Christ must be our goal. It takes humility to realize that apart from Him we can do nothing. Self-righteousness brings no gain. We stand on the righteousness of God in Christ Jesus.

> **Philippians 3:7** "But what things were gain to me, these I have counted loss for Christ."

Vine's Expository Dictionary of Biblical Words defines the verb "dedicate" as "to make new, to renew, and to initiate." The new covenant is through the blood of Jesus and represents Christ's new and living way. The noun "dedication" was first used for the annual eight days' feast known as the Feast of Dedication. It was instituted to commemorate the cleansing of the Temple from the pollutions of Antiochus Epiphanes. The lighting of the lamps was a prominent feature of this feast (Vine, 283). As we dedicate ourselves, we walk in newness of life. As we present our bodies as living sacrifices, we are cleansed from the works of the flesh.

This definition indicates the importance of consecration. We are to be the lights of the world, shining the glory of the Lord in every place. The more surrendered we are, the brighter we become. Dedication must manifest in our spirit, soul, and body. The cleansing of our body, our temple, is necessary for us to be an instrument in His hands. Our thoughts should be taken captive to the obedience of Christ; like Paul, we must be willing to lose whatever we have gained that would hinder Christ in us.

To dedicate something means to set it apart, to utilize it for a specific purpose, to give it over to a cause. When we dedicate our lives to the service of the Lord, we gradually learn to say no to whatever stops our "yes" to His call.

 Dedicating ourselves pertains to not just our surrendering our lives to the Lord but doing so with our actions.

After I was born again, my schedule didn't allow for this newfound relationship with Jesus Christ. I was a single mother, and at first glance, I was overwhelmed. There was no time to read the Word, pray or rest in Him. However, it became so crucial for me to feed my spirit man that I looked for ways to incorporate reading the Bible into my daily routine. One of those ways turned out to be my daily 30-minute bus ride to work. During that time, I would also worship Him and quiet my soul. As I closed my eyes, an awareness and appreciation of His presence helped me rest in Him and enjoy His touch.

To secure time to focus on Him alone, I would have to get up fifteen minutes earlier. While in the process of this becoming habitual, there were days that I failed to get up on time. As a result, I noticed the rest of my day didn't go as smoothly.

The challenge in dedication is the guilt that comes when distractions come; when unexpected things hinder us from spending the time we so desire with the Lord. This guilty sensation brings a sense of defeat which clouds the joy of His presence. As I cried out repeatedly to the Lord for His help and direction, I experienced His peace. He reminded me that He looks at the desires of my heart, not my devout actions. As I continue to grow in the knowledge of Him, He enables me to enjoy quality time when the "quantity" becomes unavailable.

My focus was to always make sure my children would not feel that God had become more important to me than they were. Even though He was my priority, my actions needed to express that it didn't change my love for them, but on the contrary, would help me nurture them in greater measures.

When we make room for the Lord, things change. Some friends didn't want to be around me anymore because I didn't drink with them; my conversations all focused on what the Lord was doing and how I was discovering Him. All of this was flowing out of me. I wanted to share with the world my salvation. I was blind and now I could see!

I recall that one day while riding the bus home, the Lord was ministering to me in a life-changing manner. I had been asking Him to remove any physical desires for intimacy with a man until He had a husband for me, and if He didn't have a husband for me, to remove it completely. In that ride, I suddenly heard, would you be separated unto Me? It was like the Lord was asking me to marry Him, symbolically, to be one with Him, to dedicate myself to Him. I felt a rush of living water overcome me from the top of my head to the soles of my feet. I ran home and told my daughters: "I married Jesus!" I was so filled with joy! I often tell single people to pray the same prayer.

When God gives you the desire for a mate, then He has one for you. If that desire is in your heart, after praying honestly, seek only His will and His leading will be clear.

Seasons change so we ask for His will daily and trust Him.

Luke 22:42 saying, "Father, if it is Your will, take this cup away from Me; nevertheless not My will, but Yours, be done."

We dedicate ourselves, our spouses, children, finances, jobs… they all belong to Him!

It is worth giving up whatever is required for the call on our lives; nothing comes above what God has for us. Of course, it is through continual obedience that this is established, and there are many times we miss it in the process. During these times of failure, when our walk does not match our talk, we grow. If we respond to the Holy Spirit,

His conviction will always lead us closer to the Lord. However, the condemnation of satan will push us away and cause us to remain stuck in some areas while we grow in others.

 *The* Holy Spirit reveals to heal.

He brings to light some things in our walk that not so long ago would have remained in darkness because they didn't bother us. The fact that He shows us with gentle conviction proves that He is in us to help us through this consecration process. He is so gentle and patient! He doesn't require everything of us all at once. He knows exactly what each of us needs, and our part is to yield to His leading in total obedience.

 We move forward when we recognize the areas where we have progressed.

The problems magnify in our sight and can quickly hinder the areas of victory when our eyes are on those areas that still need work.

As we dedicate every area of our lives to Him, we serve Him wholly. Our level of dedication is seen through our walk. No matter what God is calling us to do, our primary purpose is to be transformed into the image of Christ, *from glory to glory*; this transformation is demonstrated through our character.

𝒲𝒶𝓁𝓀

We cannot dedicate ourselves without dedicating our walk to Him, from step-to-step, as follows:

1. Walk in Love

The love of God, agape in Greek, is unconditional and cannot be faked by satan. It comes from our heart and is given to us by the Holy Spirit.

> **Romans 5:5** "Now hope does not disappoint, because the love of God has been poured out in our hearts by the Holy Spirit who was given to us."

 𝒲𝒽𝒶𝓉𝑒𝓋𝑒𝓇 gifts of the Holy Spirit flow through us, if we are without love, they are rendered ineffective.

> **Matthew 22:37-39** "Jesus said to him, 'YOU SHALL LOVE THE LORD YOUR GOD WITH ALL YOUR HEART, WITH ALL YOUR SOUL, AND WITH ALL YOUR MIND.' This is the first and great commandment. And the second is like it: 'YOU SHALL LOVE YOUR NEIGHBOR AS YOURSELF.'"

Compassion flows out of love, and love conquers all, including fear which the enemy uses to hinder our walk. The more we grow in love, the less we retract. The degree to which we understand and receive His love for us, and what He did because of it, is the degree to which we will love Him and therefore be able to love others and ourselves.

1 John 4:19 "We love Him because He first loved us."

When we love God and our neighbor but not ourselves, or love our neighbor and ourselves but not God, or we love God, ourselves, and not our neighbor, we open a door to the enemy. These three areas of love must be covered: God, our neighbor, and ourselves. As we allow the Lord to heal our broken heart, we become whole. There's nothing we can do for God to cause Him to love us more, or less.

1 John 4:18 "There is no fear in love; but perfect love casts out fear, because fear involves torment. But he who fears has not been made perfect in love."

Walking in love comes first before walking in truth and in the Spirit. It is the springboard to the manifestation of all the fruit of the Spirit, and the evidence of our salvation. Love also helps us grow into Him in all things. God is love.

Ephesians 4:15 "but, speaking the truth in love, may grow up in all things into Him who is the head, Christ."

We should therefore pray for more love to manifest through us everywhere we go.

The fruit of the Holy Spirit comes before the gifts.

We should love one another in deed and in truth. When we truly walk in love, we will speak and walk in truth as He has.

2. Walk in Truth

This increasing transformation carries another evidence of character: integrity.

 Integrity will meet a prosperity that will last for eternity.

True prosperity in all areas of our lives will flourish as we do all in view of our eternal destiny. Many desires the prosperity of their finances, but not of their souls which in turn hinders their health. God's provision is for wholeness and as we seek first the kingdom, all necessary needs are met.

> **3 John 2-4** "Beloved, I pray that you may prosper in all things and be in health, just as your soul prospers. For I rejoiced greatly when brethren came and testified of the truth that is in you, just as you walk in the truth. I have no greater joy than to hear that my children walk in truth."

We can prosper in truth in every area of our lives, and as prosperity is reached, that truth is manifested. The Greek for prosper is *eudeo,* which means to succeed. We are being restored to an unbroken state; to the likeness of Christ. Our transformation by the renewing of our mind can be defined as the prosperity of our soul. This wholeness is directly connected with truth in all areas of our lives. As ambassadors of Christ, the integrity we walk in positions us to receive an increase in all areas.

Webster's definition of integrity includes:

1   Wholeness; entireness; unbroken state. The Constitution of the United States guarantees to each state the integrity of its territories. The contracting parties guarantee the integrity of the empire.

2   The entire, unimpaired state of anything, particularly of the mind; moral soundness or purity; incorruptness; uprightness; honesty. Integrity comprehends the whole moral character but has a special reference to uprightness in mutual dealings, transfers of property, and agencies for others.

3   Purity; genuine, unadulterated, unimpaired state; as the integrity of language.

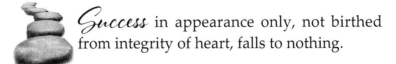 *Success* in appearance only, not birthed from integrity of heart, falls to nothing.

As we heed the conviction of the Holy Spirit and yield to His guidance, we are reformed in all areas where we have lied, stretched, omitted, hidden, twisted, or hindered truth to gain something. We see a great exhibit of restoration. This applies to relationships, businesses, ministries, and any other fields where growth has come but was not founded upon truth. Confession and repentance cleanse past errors, and forgiveness opens a door to the "much more" of God. "Ishmael prosperity," what is brought forth by the flesh, needs to be turned over to God so that "Isaac prosperity" can be brought forth and released by the Spirit. To walk in our future, we must walk in truth in all areas of our lives. Many secret sins are being revealed, and many will be healed. God desires to entrust much more into our lives. As we take heed to this word, many other words spoken over our lives can come to pass.

> **Proverbs 19:1** "Better is the poor who walks in his integrity Than one who is perverse in his lips, and is a fool."

It also reaches future generations. Part of the inheritance we leave is integrity of our hearts; our children are linked to it.

> **Proverbs 20:7** "The righteous man walks in his integrity; His children are blessed after him."

In looking at our heart, can God choose us as He did David?

Psalms 78:70-72 "He also chose David His servant And took him from the sheepfolds; From following the ewes that had young He brought him, To shepherd Jacob His people, And Israel His inheritance. So he shepherded them according to the integrity of his heart, And guided them by the skillfulness of his hands."

To walk in truth brings freedom from lies, lack, oppression, depression, bondage, and many other things that hinder our walking in divine identity. We dedicate what comes into our hands so that our hands remain clean, and through us God is glorified!

> **John 17:17** "Sanctify them by Your truth. Your word is truth."

3. Walk in the Spirit

It becomes evident that we move in the Spirit when the inward work of the Holy Spirit is revealed outwardly.

 What is on the inside comes out under pressure.

Stressful situations are allowed by God to bring to the surface what still needs to be healed. The opposite is true of the Spirit-led life: the fruit of the Spirit comes forth when testing demonstrates what has been perfected in hidden places. The fruit is exhibited by what has taken place on the inside.

Galatians 5:22-26 "But the fruit of the Spirit is love, joy, peace, longsuffering, kindness, goodness, faithfulness, gentleness, self-control. Against such there is no law. And those who are Christ's have crucified the flesh with its passions and desires. If we live in the Spirit, let us also walk in the Spirit. Let us not become conceited, provoking one another, envying one another."

 The deep work of the Spirit happens in the secret place. It cannot be faked or fabricated. We bear fruit; we cannot create it.

As we abide in Him and yield to His working in us, He can work through us. What is private is revealed in public.

The Spirit of Christ abiding in us results in an outflow of His characteristics. They increase as our flesh decreases. As the scripture indicates, the fruit is for those who are Christ's; who have crucified the flesh with its affections and lusts. Thus, to the degree in which we identify with His crucifixion, we can identify with His resurrection. The life of the Spirit emanates from the death of the flesh.

Galatians 5:16 "I say then: Walk in the Spirit, and you shall not fulfill the lust of the flesh."

The new creation we are in Christ manifests as the old man remains dead. When we walk in the Spirit, His character overflows. It eliminates vain glory and provoking or envying one another.

From faith to faith, we seek less of our flesh so that more of His Spirit can flow through us. Could this be spiritual maturity?

Watch

When we walk increasingly in love, in truth and in the spirit, we learn to guard against three of the most devastating attitudes our carnal nature carries: comparing, criticizing, and complaining. These traits give place to esteeming, exhorting, and contentment.

1. Comparing

Comparing happens naturally because we are inclined to relate to others to define ourselves. In Christ, we learn to accept ourselves as the Lord does and see Jesus as the image we are being transformed into, and no one else. When we compare ourselves to others, we belittle who we are or esteem ourselves higher than others instead of celebrating each other and rejoicing in our differences. This applies not just to who we are, but also to what we have. What we possess materially doesn't place us in an inferior or superior position to others. We give God glory in all situations and for all material things!

The act of comparing ourselves with others encompasses judgmentalism that comes from walking by sight. It can result in jealousy and envy for something we assume is better. It has been said "the grass is greener on the other side." We are not to look at the outward appearance. The only thing to compare are the prices when shopping, the neighborhoods when moving, the churches when worshipping and so forth, not the people. We see God's will in all things. In contrast, people should be viewed as unique and God's workmanship.

We also are not to compare today with our yesterdays when we thought we had more success and happiness; or compare our today with our tomorrow when we think we will have accomplished more. This brings a sense of regret or defeat. It is only beneficial when assessing goals and planning as we are led by the Lord.

We also shouldn't compare ourselves with others who are in the same profession. We individually abide in Christ, the vine. We are the branches and each one of us matters.

 We do not compete with others, but we complete one another.

When we move into a new career, relationship, ministry or any type of novel situation, we dedicate ourselves and those circumstances to Him. It might not appear to be as "great" as the last thing, but when it's dedicated, it becomes fresh in Him and we can expect the best, and nothing less! As a child of the Most High God, we always measure up. We praise God for who and where we are and trust Him for all He is doing in our lives.

2. Criticizing

All of us are criticized at one time or another whether known or unknown to us. Others point out our faults and shortcomings in a disapproving way. Words can bring life or death. Criticism especially hurts when it comes from someone we care for, and when this happens, we must bring the pain to the Lord and forgive them. We must not pick up an offense but reject it immediately. When we know the person, it is helpful to ask ourselves, *what was the intent of their heart? Was it to build up and edify us? Was it spoken out of concern for us?* We confront them with an attitude of resolution and reconciliation when possible.

We ask the Lord to help us not to criticize others. As we learn to walk in love, when we are led by the Holy Spirit to speak a truth to someone else, it will come with love and tenderness. As we seek to walk in truth, we will make sure we have all the needed information about a situation and seek accurate discernment so that we can help others effectively.

As our mind is renewed by the Word of God, we don't criticize ourselves as often. We learn to take our thoughts captive to the obedience of Christ. We remember how much God loves us and stop focusing on our faults. We rejoice for who God made us to be.

 If I criticize who I am, I criticize God Himself.

We trust the Lord and reject the list of all the wrongs we see in ourselves. We believe the truth: we are accepted by God, amen?

3. Complaining

Complaining hinders our moving forward. A murmuring, complaining spirit is displeasing to the Lord. It is normal to express grief and sorrow or share something that is happening in our lives. It is not normal to grumble, accuse, blame, speak negatively and not acknowledge anything positive.

To complain means to express dissatisfaction or annoyance about a situation or a person. When we complain we are telling God we don't like what He is allowing. We are displeased with Him and frustrated with the cup He has placed in our hands. This hinders our prayer of faith. We can trust that He will be glorified through all things.

It is even more destructive when complaining about people and not things. It leads to gossip and fuels the works of the enemy. Our war is not against flesh and blood and the weapons of our warfare are mighty through God! Instead of complaining we should walk in authority against every opposition, in the name of Jesus!

Complaining comes from a spirit of fear which is conquered as the Lord brings freedom. When we want to help those who are being battled in this area, we should lead them to the awareness of what the Lord has already done.

We shine the light in the darkness and lift them up with affirming words of life, hope and trust.

We encourage them through the expression of our faith. We help one another stand by faith.

In conclusion, regarding this valuable stepping stone, we seek to stay committed to the Lord. We also commit what He leads us to do into His hands. Proverbs 16:3 tells us, "Commit your works to the Lord, And your thoughts will be established." Dedication is a daily spiritual exercise and by God's grace we progress in it, *from glory to glory*!

Reflection

- What are some things you need to dedicate to answer the call?

- Recall a time when it was challenging to walk in love. How did the Lord help you? How about when walking in truth?

- What helps or hinders you to not compare yourself with others?

- How did you handle criticism? What did you learn that helps you now and will in the future?

- How do you keep from complaining when your circumstances appear hopeless?

Action steps

1 Make a list of what you are dedicating to the Lord today.

2 Dedicate everything on that list to Him and partake communion.

3 Write down what the Holy Spirit is showing you to watch for as you continue to answer the call of God on your life.

Prayer

Father,

I dedicate myself to You, all that I am and all that I have for Your use, as You will! Please enable me to keep a consecrated life. Teach me how to walk in love, in truth and in the Spirit. Guard me against comparing, criticizing and complaining. Help me to be quick to recognize my weaknesses and give me the ability to confront conflicts. I yield myself to You and rest in Your loving care. I surrender my will to Yours. I am Your vessel and love You so much, in Jesus' name.

Amen.

CHAPTER 4

Philippians 3:13-14 *"Brethren, I do not count myself to have apprehended: but this one thing I do, forgetting those things which are behind and reaching forward to those things which are ahead, I press toward the goal for the prize of the upward call of God in Christ Jesus."*

DESTINATION

THIS STEPPING STONE, Destination, helps assure us that even when we don't know where we are heading, we can trust His leading, step-by-step, *from glory to glory!* The firm foundation we established through Death, Discipleship and Dedication gives us more confidence in God and guards us from deception.

 We enjoy the journey because it's part of our destiny, regardless of the destination.

How did Paul reach beyond his reach? How can we?

Apprehend
We must never assume we have arrived while we continue to pursue our calling.

 Constantly knowing that there is more to attain is mandatory for growth.

When we recognize we have not yet reached our full potential, we seek after it with humility and reverence to God's will. Like Paul states:

Philippians 3:12 "Not as though I had already attained, either were already perfect: but I follow after, if that I may apprehend that for which also I am apprehended of Christ Jesus." (KJV)

Apprehended comes from the Greek word *katalambano*, which comes from the word kata, meaning down, against, or according to; and the word *lambano*, meaning to take or receive. Together they mean to lay hold of as to make one's own, to obtain, to take into one's self, to appropriate, to seize upon or to take possession of.

Understanding that we have not chosen Christ Jesus, but He has chosen us, breaks pride and self-reliance. When I look at my past and can see God's hand on me before I knew Him, I stand in awe of His care. He apprehended me first, I did not apprehend Him. The full purpose for which I am His is yet to unfold. We are His workmanship, created in Him for good works indeed.

Ephesians 2:10 "For we are His workmanship, created in Christ Jesus for good works, which God prepared beforehand that we should walk in them."

Christ laid hold of us through the cross. All that He purchased for us on Calvary we must appropriate in our lives.

Our position in Him determines our provision.

To possess what He has for us requires a continual pursuit of those things that are above and not beneath; the heavenly, not the earthly. We have a glimmering view of it and are blessed with hope in our inheritance. We aim to lay hold of what He has laid hold of us for even though we do not know all that it entails.

Therefore, this first observation is the basis of our walk. We cannot put God in a box. Assuming we know all things and insisting on doing what we thought we were called to do will cause us to be stuck. Paul counts on God taking him from *glory to glory*. He knows he has not yet apprehended all for which God has apprehended him. We all go forth and grow progressively *from glory to glory*.

No matter what we think God is doing, we find out He is doing so much more. We seek to obey His leading step-by-step even though we don't always understand His plan. We trust He knows our future and learn to rest in Him. We do not see the full picture as He does. To us, it looks like a dot-to-dot game. As the dots are connected, the picture gets clearer. When we look at our past, we recognize some things God has orchestrated for our good. When we realize what He has done, and we grow in the knowledge of who He is and what He can do. He is omniscient (all knowing), omnipotent (all powerful), and omnipresent (everywhere at the same time). His faithfulness fills our hearts with gratitude.

 Some events in our lives are turning points to unexpected outcomes.

For example, years ago I worked as a waitress in a French restaurant in Denver, Colorado, called Le Central. As a single mother, I would take on double shifts to make ends meet because I didn't have any other way to provide for my daughters. To all appearances this was a dead-end job; no advancement or prospective change appeared possible. I could not imagine relief from the long hours, many evenings and weekends away from home, and physical exhaustion. This situation appeared to have no future.

One day, during a busy Friday night shift, I approached a table occupied by two couples with no time to pay attention to who they were or engage in a conversation. I greeted them with "Bonjour, I'm Joelle. What may I serve you tonight?" I took their order in haste and rushed to the next table. I attended to their requests in my regular friendly fashion without knowing they were divine connections to a brighter future.

I first brought their drinks silently. When I took their salads to them, I said, "Bon appétit!" and after serving their main entrees, "Enjoy, may I get you anything else?" I returned a few minutes later and asked, "How is everything?" They replied, "delicious." One of the gentlemen said, "It's great. What a delightful accent, I would love for you to answer our phones at the office." I understood his request as a compliment and nothing further. I just smiled and said, "Oh, thank you!" When I came back to clear their plates, he said, "I'm serious you know. Would you be interested?" I looked at his wife thinking she would give me the assurance of the seriousness and reality of his appeal. She smiled and said, "My husband is serious." I turned to the other couple, and they shook their heads yes. All I could say was, "Oh, really?" He answered, "Yes, our Law Firm is Edwyn and Stevenson and we have an opening for a receptionist. You would just need to pass a light typing and aptitude test." The shock of this unexpected opportunity made me speechless. He could tell my surprise and as he pulled something out of his wallet, he said, "Here is my card. Call to set up the appointment in a couple of weeks. We are looking to hire at the beginning of October." I took the card and said, "Thank you so much! I so appreciate it."

I rushed to the kitchen and amid the frantic rush of the night, I yelled, "Does anyone have a typewriter? I need to learn how to type." Everyone looked at me with wonder and continued their tasks without answering me. I continued attending to my tables but could barely focus on my duties. My spirit suddenly leaped with hope and excitement. At the end of the shift, another server approached me. "I have a typewriter you can use." "Thank you so much. I'm going to apply for this receptionist job in a couple of weeks and I need to pass a light typing test." He proceeded to laugh but when he saw the determination in my eyes, he just responded, "Good luck". *Luck*, I thought, *this is going to take an act of God! Am I out of my mind? Is it possible?* When I got home that night I suddenly realized what had happened. It was surreal. Fear gripped me, *what am I thinking? When am I going to have time to learn? Is my English good enough?* I also sensed a resolve to go for it with every ounce of my being. The possibility of being free from the place where I felt stuck overcame all doubts and hesitations.

For two weeks I practiced whenever I could, using a book I found in a library. I learned the typewriter keys, where to put my fingers and how to type! When the appointment time came, the confidence I had gained from that little training helped me walk in as though I knew what I was doing. How supernatural! The test revealed I could type 30 words a minute, not much in comparison to the average 70 words per minute. Thanks to the English I studied in school in France, the aptitude test came back 65 out of 100. One of the attorneys led me to a separate room to role play answering the phone, and then to a conference room to meet with the other partner. They explained the specific duties of the position, the pay of $800 a month, the commitment they expected, and the review they gave quarterly. He then asked, "Why would you say you are the right person for this position?" I answered, "Because I would give it my all and learn whatever is necessary to do the job well. I sure wouldn't take a job that paid less than what I've been earning if I didn't believe I could do it. Please give me a chance to prove myself to you." Even though it would mean taking a pay cut, having this job would allow me to be with my children in the evening and eventually on weekends too. At the beginning, I would still work on some weekends to make up for the difference in pay. What an opportunity!

A few days later I was offered the position. In my life, I've had many happenings like this where God would open a door I didn't know existed. I apprehended that for which Christ apprehended me by learning with each step to trust Him for the unseen and follow Him wholeheartedly. I didn't always succeed, but to this day I know I have not yet arrived, and I look forward to discovering what the Lord has prepared for me.

 At times, we assume the destination we have reached is final, only to realize it's a page turner to the next chapter in our story.

We cannot place a period where God writes a comma, and vice versa. Some relationships that appear to be permanent turn out to be temporary, and others we thought would be temporary become permanent.

Stepping stones pave our walk of faith.

We can trust God and praise Him in every place, regardless of what we see.

Forget

Paul declared that there was one thing that he continually did – he forgot those things that were behind.

> **Philippians 3:13** "Brethren, I do not count myself to have apprehended: but this one thing I do, forgetting those things which are behind and reaching forward to those things which are ahead."

Forgetting, in this context, means to loose from one's mind, to neglect, no longer care for a specific thing. What are we to forget?

 We put out of our mind our failures and mistakes through forgiveness.

We let go of the negative influence some past events hold on our present pursuits. We also forget our successes. The ways we accomplished an assignment in the past might not necessarily work for what we are doing now or what lay ahead of us. There is a tendency to trust what was successful in the past rather than inquire of the Lord. However, the directives may or may not remain the same. This is true not only for what we have done ourselves, but also in relation to what others have completed. To copy what someone else has done and think we will obtain the same results is dangerous because each person is designed and ordained by God for specific works that only they can do.

When we are involved in an area the Lord called us to, we should periodically seek Him to reaffirm the call. It's easy to get comfortable in an area and assume that what He led us to do thirty years ago, He still wants us to do. We must ask Him, "Am I still in your will?" "Is there something else you would like me to do?" "Is there anything or anyone I need to let go of to be ready for what you have ahead of me?" The Holy Spirit helps us transform our habits and changes our desires. It takes courage to forget our old ways or even the ways of others.

When the Lord directed me to start a church, I hesitated aware of the challenges for women in leadership until I knew for sure it was His will and then waited for His timing. I first looked at the ways others established churches thinking that would help me know what to do, but the opposite happened. I found myself confused, and I had no peace. I sought His will in prayer and heard, *seek me for the specific instructions on the foundation of the ministry I'm calling you to launch.* "Lord how should the worship time of the service be orchestrated?" *Use songs on cassette: the people will be the worship team.* "Lord, how do I handle the collection of tithes and offerings?" *Trust me for the finances. Place a few baskets in the back and I will lead the people in their giving.*

often inquire, "Lord is this still the way you want this or that to be done?"

Three years later, while pondering, "Lord, what you asked me to do seems to be going well but I feel something is not flowing as it should. What am I missing?" I will never forget the valuable lesson the answer carried, *you are doing the right thing, at the right time but in the wrong territory.* I fell on my knees in repentance. "Oh, Lord I sought your will about the what, the when but not the where! Please forgive me. What should I do now?" *Fast and pray and I will show you the territory,* He replied after a few hours at His feet. At that time, the church's location was in Arvada on the west side of Denver. That location had made sense because it was close to my job as an accountant for a printing company. What may be logical in the natural doesn't necessarily match the supernatural. I stood in front of the congregation the following Sunday humbly sharing what I had heard, and we began the search process with fasting and prayer. The territory turned out to be in Aurora on the east side of Denver. Since then I ask the Lord, "Am I still doing the right thing? Am I still in the right territory? Is it your timing for something different?" Oh, the grace of God! He is so faithful. He sees our hearts and turns our mistakes into greater glory.

The "what" represents the action we are led to take: move to a city, open a ministry, a business, buy a house, a car, settle down in a relationship and so forth. The "when" is the timing. When the timing is not of God, He will close the doors when our hearts are for His will above all. When His timing does come, it is accompanied by peace and an easy flow. Only He knows the preparation we still need to take us into a place of prospering in the calling. It brings problems when we make some things happen before God's opportune time. The "where" is the territory. The place is usually not obvious. For me, I thought knowing the location was enough. For the radio program, the station was the territory to seek after. For purchasing items like the chairs for the church, the company represented the territory. God worked it out for the good by teaching me how important it is to wait on Him in all three areas. I pray and trust He will lead you as you read about this lesson to ask and keep asking. Hallelujah!

To establish the ministry in the next place, I needed to forgive myself for the error and loose it from my mind. Satan kept sending fiery darts of guilt and self-condemnation. I thought, *I missed God before in that area, how can I be sure of what I hear now?* The Lord knows our humanity, and He reassures us of His higher ways. By His grace, He helped me to forgive myself and receive His forgiveness. Only then could I forget my past mistakes and obey my new instructions. The Lord taught me this lesson, and so many others, in such a way that it continues to fill my heart with gratitude. This is not a onetime test. It's repeated over and over as we learn to obey Him, *from glory to glory!*

The Spirit of Christ is a pioneer spirit. There is newness of life in doing what He calls us to do. He gives us our daily bread and does not want us to use yesterday's manna.

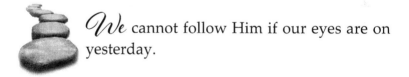

We cannot follow Him if our eyes are on yesterday.

What happened then can hinder our future if we let it. Forgetting is necessary.

Reach Forth

Paul then says that reaching forth must be done to forget. We get this picture of Paul letting go of something that is behind him to lay hold of what is before him. Oftentimes, when we do not know there is something ahead of us, we hang on to the past. We do this because what is in front of us is beyond our reach in the natural and requires a stretching forth, a pulling forward, an assurance of the evidence of the things not seen.

 It is in the forgetting that we can do the reaching. Both actions are necessary.

What we reach for must be more important to us than what we are required to let go of to move forward. This is the point where the battle rages. Because we are familiar and comfortable with what needs to be removed, it is difficult to move into an unknown area. We often freeze in our steps and fear intervenes. We wait for some proof that what is to come will turn out all right but all we get is more doubt. Our trust cannot be in what we know, but in who we know. When we know Him, our Master Jesus Christ, we will make every effort necessary to obey Him. If we are persistent in our endeavors God will always lead us to move.

He will allow circumstances to push us forward. If we start anything counting on ourselves, then when difficulties arise we doubt His help because we know deep inside that we were asking Him to follow us instead of us following

Him. Praise Him forevermore that even in this case He pulls us out of our prideful decisions when we count on His mercy and grace. The key is to continue seeking His will rather than taking things for granted. Let us remember not to step too soon into a situation when we have grown weary in waiting on God. Presumption is as much a sin as rebellion. *Rebellion* is not doing what we know God has told us to do. *Presumption* means to believe we can do what He told us to do in our own way and with our own abilities.

> **Galatians 3:3** "Are you so foolish? Having begun in the Spirit, are you now being made perfect by the flesh?"

Another obstacle in reaching forth is judging what lies ahead as being too small or unimportant. It is interesting that God tests our hearts by putting something small in front of us to see what we will do with it. The enemy's tactic is to intensify what he puts in our way when in fact it is small and powerless.

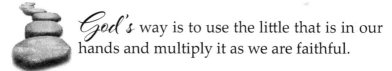

God's way is to use the little that is in our hands and multiply it as we are faithful.

He then gives us much more. I discovered that our little is much in His hands. In obeying what He has asked me to do, I realized that nothing ever was as it first appeared. For example, reaching out to one person was connected to many others. When I helped another minister in need, a connection to an international ministry opened. Going out of my way to obey simple instructions placed me in the right position for another matter. Oh, that we may never limit God with what we can see!

After we found the right territory, we held services in a hotel. After a few months, the need to open a food bank was laid upon my heart. A room for rent became available not far from the hotel. I remembered the lesson and prayed, "Lord is this the right thing to do at this time, and is this the right territory?" After hearing clearly His yes and receiving confirmation, we contacted the owner to inquire about a lease and set up a meeting. The front room occupied around 800 square feet. In its rear, a warehouse could be utilized to store the food items. As I observed each room, I began sensing the existence of more space. A condemned door on the east side of the wall caught my attention. I placed my hand on it and an excitement stirred in my spirit. I questioned the owner, "is there anything else available?" He replied, "only a warehouse full of junk, old cars and unused equipment." I heard this request come out of my mouth, "Can I see It?"

When I looked inside that warehouse I didn't see the junk, I saw a beautiful sanctuary! The discovery of this hidden treasure exceeded all my expectations. For a few days I prayed fervently. I received no check marks, no hesitation, total peace and clear direction from the Lord. He led me to take the next step of faith, call the landlord and say, "yes to both places." We reach for the more the Lord has kept for us when we are faithful with the little.

Another aspect of reaching is to move forward with "the little," yet always having the "much more" in view. Decisions cannot be made with subtraction in our calculations. Because God is a God of multiplication, we should expect something to grow. For example, in setting up phones for an office with four people, we should buy a system to which lines can be added, not a phone system that will only accommodate four employees.

What we reach for will require withdrawals from deposits God has already made in our lives. The provision needed for what He has us reach for will come when it is needed, not before. There are deposits made in our lives for things that are yet to come.

1 Corinthians 2:9 says, "But as it is written: Eye has not seen, nor ear heard, Nor have entered into the heart of man The things which God has prepared for those who love Him."

God sees the end from the beginning and waters our vineyard of today with the harvest of tomorrow in view.

Accountability is defined as the state of being liable to answer for one's conduct; liability to give an account and to receive reward or punishment for actions. We are accountable to God and will explain to Him what we have done with what He deposited into our lives at the judgment seat of Christ. Our stewardship matters to our success in Him. Paul did what he did with eternity in view, and we should do the same. We should also surround ourselves with people to whom we can be *accountable*.

Because of this, in reaching for what God has apprehended me for, I remind myself of two basic wisdom keys:

The first is: *haste makes waste.* Anything I must do in a hurry brings a check in my spirit. If I do not have time to consult with the Lord as His co-laborer, then it cannot be from Him. Now this is different from the times when the Spirit of the Lord comes upon me to move suddenly. In those times, He moves so fast that it's only afterwards that I realize what He has done. The peace and surety that come cannot be faked by satan, our adversary. Sometimes responding and acting quickly seems to be right because of our need to help ourselves or others. We assume it is okay with the Lord without making sure. Fruitfulness comes as we seek God.

The second is: *when in doubt, don't.* We cannot move in fear and faith at the same time. If I have any doubt about the direction I am to take, I stop, pray, and ask for divine wisdom as instructed in James 1:5, "If any of you lacks wisdom, let him ask of God, who gives to all liberally and without reproach, and it will be given to him." Divine wisdom is accompanied by peace and confidence. It contains no check marks, confusion or fear. Even five percent doubt signals us to wait. Sometimes a lack of perfect peace doesn't mean something is not from God. It just means more factors are to be brought into the situation to bring that one hundred percent peace. We wait and trust Him to lead us as He wills.

Finally, Paul knew that using keys of the world would not open doors of the kingdom. Those doors are only accessible with kingdom principles. When God gives us a vision, He also releases the instructions along with the "unction to function" in every detail, step-by-step. There are several examples in the Bible where people were given specifics: Noah for constructing the ark and Solomon for building the temple. We can trust Him to do the same for us.

Rest assured that God can speak loud enough for us to hear Him, and as we acknowledge Him in all our ways, He directs our paths.

> **Proverbs 3:5-6** "Trust in the LORD with all your heart, And lean not on your own understanding; In all your ways acknowledge Him, And He shall direct your paths."

In observing Paul's life and many others in the Bible, we can be encouraged that if God used them, He can surely use us. The testimony of God is greater when we are not qualified, and He qualifies us. It has been said that God does not call the qualified but qualifies the called: by His grace we are called. By walking into what He has already done for us and placing our faith in Him and not in ourselves, we are not only called but chosen.

When something we have reached for falls to nothing, we should rejoice.

 Not only the steps, but also the stops, are ordered by God.

Over the years I have had to remind myself often of what is written in:

> **Acts 5:38-39** "And now I say to you, keep away from these men and let them alone; for if this plan or this work is of men, it will come to nothing; but if it is of God, ye cannot overthrow it - lest you even be found to fight against God."

So, if a plan or a work is of men and not of God, it will come to nothing. But if the work is of God, I trust that whatever battles are coming my way are against Him and not me. The battle is then His, and I rest. What is of God cannot be overthrown! Hallelujah!

Philippians 3:14 "I press toward the goal for the prize of the upward call of God in Christ Jesus."

 When we try to obtain the prize of the high calling of God in Christ Jesus, the decisions we make, and the directions we take, will be heaven bound.

Our eyes are on the incorruptible crown, the crown of life, righteousness, and glory that does not fade away. We are called to a glorious kingdom.

 When we realize the greater glory lies ahead, all the steps in between will be from one level of glory to another.

Reflection

- Look back at some of the big pictures in your life (your marriage, church, ministry, the house you live in, etc.) and think back on the events (dots) that made the big picture whole.

- What helps you in the "step-by-step" concept?

- Recall an example where either the thing (what), the time (when) or the territory (where) was incorrect? How did you move forward?

- In reaching forth, what has been hindering you the most and what progress have you been making with the help of the Holy Spirit?

- Do you remember the healing you walked in after forgiving yourself for making a wrong decision? How did you then regain assurance in your steps?

Action Steps

1 Write down what your dots look like. What bigger picture do you hope it connects to?

2 Make a list of what you still need to forget.

3 Keep a journal (if you don't have one), on the decisions you make using the wisdom keys described in this chapter.

Prayer

Father,

I thank You for leading me to my destination and I rejoice for everything You have for me. I trust You with what I cannot see, from faith to faith. I forget those things that are behind, so I can reach for Your best. Please forgive me for the decisions I made without seeking Your guidance. Help me guard against haste, look for accountability and follow Your peace with every step I take. I apprehend all that You have apprehended me for. Have Your way, I pray, in Jesus' name.

Amen.

CHAPTER 5

James 1:2-4 *"My brethren, count it all joy when you fall into various trials, knowing that the testing of your faith produces patience. But let patience have its perfect work, that you may be perfect and complete, lacking nothing."*

DIVERSE TRIALS

As we obey the call of God on our lives, unforeseen difficulties arise. This stepping stone, diverse trials, helps us overcome these obstacles. Our ability to win these battles relates to our foreseeing trials as launching pads for our purpose. To foresee means we have *accounted* for it to happen. It doesn't say *if*, it says *when* because it is to be expected.

 If we count the cost accurately, unexpected trials will be part of expected triumphs.

The devil fighting us from the opposite direction is confirmation that are going in the right direction.

Our Battles

 The battles we face are not coming in opposition to where we are, but to where we are going.

When we look at our current state, we do not understand the intensity of the war that comes against us. It is hard to imagine how what we have can cause such an uproar. Our opponent tries to stop the manifestation of the greater One who is in us, Christ Jesus. The more the anointing increases in and through us, the more hindrances are to be expected.

If the devil can cause us to focus on problems related to relationships, jobs, money, material things, or other natural happenings, the release of the anointing becomes hindered.

 satan throws fiery darts aimed at the outward to hinder the inward.

He is most threatened when the Greater One who is within us is free to move. As we keep our eyes on the Lord, we walk by faith and not by sight. The battle then is truly the Lord's, and the explosion of His glory comes forth in His timing to destroy every mountain and every yoke that tries to slow us down. Victory is already ours!

When we realize the war is about stopping the glory within us from bursting forth, the strength of the Lord intensifies. The Holy Spirit empowers us to face all trials with His ability, and we no longer react as we did previously. Instead of fighting against flesh and blood, we can perceive what is happening in the spiritual realm and come against it specifically. Fleshly battles are replaced with spiritual battles attacking the enemy directly, in the name of Jesus.

When we face a battle, we ask ourselves: "What is the real reason for this battle?"

 When we perceive the actual motive behind an action, we no longer waste time fighting what appears to be, but address what truly needs to be overcome.

I experienced this in various areas right after I surrendered my life to the Lord. People around me would pick up offense for no apparent reason. They would be short with me, try to avoid me or appear to be angry. I would try to figure out what I had done, or not done; said, or not said. I confronted people lovingly and asked them if there was anything wrong, and if so, to please forgive me. Their answer was always no, or nothing, but their actions spoke the opposite. It came through family members as well as strangers. I could feel tension and warfare but couldn't pinpoint the reason. This truth became so clear to me:

> **Ephesians 6:12** "For we do not wrestle against flesh and blood, but against principalities, against powers, against the rulers of the darkness of this age, against spiritual hosts of wickedness in the heavenly places."

The knowledge of this truth brought me freedom in these situations. I began growing in the understanding of the spiritual realm and learned they could only be confronted in and with the Spirit of God. I prayed against these principalities, powers, rulers of the darkness of this world and against wickedness in high places, and I no longer let them steal my joy and peace. On the contrary, I volunteered with a greater passion and grew in discipleship. We must always be aware of the spiritual warfare we face.

Attacks will come unexpectedly from various sources through three main venues: the world, the flesh and the devil. The trials James refers come in a variety of areas. The key word is various.

> **James 1:2** "My brethren, count it all joy when you fall into various trials,"

Diversity will come with adversity. The enemy will try to surprise us so that we do not see him coming. If we are used to warring in one area only, we do not watch in another. One might be free from an addiction to alcohol for years and suddenly be battled with it again, or with a new temptation such as a spirit of lust. Another might face temptation in finances when it had never been an issue. As we walk in our healing in areas of the soul, our bodies will come under attack. Fiery darts may stab us in our backs, heads or other areas without any warning. Because of our knowledge of their source, and our trust in the victory we possess in Christ, we can war effectively.

Starting the church, Glory to Glory Christian Center, came with total peace from the Lord… but I encountered war from outside opposition. The objection to my leadership and preaching as a woman surprised me because I erroneously thought people in the Body of Christ walked in an understanding and revelation of the freedom we have in Christ. Interestingly, it was because the women in the Corinthian Church had discovered freedom in the gospel and were learning to flow in it that they were deemed out of order and Paul reprimanded them. The level in which we realize it is God Himself who calls us to do something, is the level in which we will be able to stand in our place of obedience.

I often received threatening calls and was confronted with people cursing me right before a sermon on a Sunday morning. A few times, people were used by our adversary to sow discord and strife while fueling lies. One morning before service, a six-foot-long black snake, five inches wide, was laid on the threshold of the front door. These attacks only made way for the Lord to teach me about the bypass anointing and increased the Teflon anointing, so the fiery darts would not stick to me.

When our adversary tries to come against the anointing so that it decreases, the opposite occurs, it increases.

> **1 John 4:4** "You are of God, little children, and have overcome them, because He who is in you is greater than he who is in the world."

We always need to watch and pray. On a battlefield it is important to know when to fire, when not to fire, when to hide, and how to proceed. When the commander gives us instructions, we are to follow them no questions asked. The tactics are similar in spiritual warfare. Our King knows what to do to establish His kingdom. We receive specific directives and obey them even if we don't see the end results like He does …so perfectly.

Our Weapons

> **2 Corinthians** 10:3-4 "For though we walk in the flesh, we do not war according to the flesh. For the weapons of our warfare are not carnal but mighty in God for pulling down strongholds."

We fight our battles with spiritual weapons. The Holy Spirit sharpens our Sword of the Spirit, which is the Word of God, and helps us with our most valuable tools: worship and prayer.

Worship takes us into a higher realm where our fighting can be done from above, not beneath.

All things are under our feet and we quench all the fiery darts of satan, our adversary, by stepping on every lie. It is important to have a specific scripture for a specific situation. It is then that the unspeakable joy, full of glory, floods our souls. When we war in the flesh we become agitated, yell, express anger, say things we do not mean and become worn out quickly with nothing accomplished. It's when we take the time to be with the Lord that we can confront conflicts with the fruit of the Spirit. We speak words of life, not death. When we war in the Spirit, we must know how to wait until we can battle by, and with, the Spirit.

Intimacy in worship becomes our most viable preparation point. It is in our worship that the war is won; the place in which we become filled with the right ammunition and receive instructions. We are strengthened by Him and empowered with His might. It takes time to enter His presence when we are battled. We press through no matter how long it takes, shake the dust off our feet and praise Him until we have the breakthrough. Worship cannot be offered apart from prayer. So how do we pray?

 In worship, what we have received through the cross is revealed. In prayer, we learn how to use what we have.

Through it we obtain directions on where to aim our sword, the Word of God. Praying in the Spirit keeps us edified and the enemy at bay.

It is also through prayer that our armor: our helmet of salvation, the breastplate of righteousness, the belt of truth, shoes for the preparation of the gospel of peace, shield of faith and sword of the Spirit are polished with His anointing.

Prayer doesn't focus on asking God to fulfill our personal needs, but centers on hearing His strategies for battle. It should be: "What is it that *you* want, Lord? What can I do for *you*? What is *your* heart? What is *your* will?" We have a personal relationship with our God and communicating with Him is how we grow into the knowledge of Him.

Worship and prayer are two major keys to the kingdom. The result of our worship and prayer is always obedience.

It was only a couple of weeks after moving into a duplex that I encountered spiritual warfare in a terrifying manner. The two-story property from around 1950 held a depressing sense in each room. On the main floor, a murphy bed was in the living room to the side of the kitchen, and I slept there while the upstairs room was being set up. At 9:30 one evening, I had just finished preparing for bed and sensed the same heaviness I noticed the first time I walked into the house. I prayed, Lord, thank you for your presence and protection. With no training in spiritual warfare, I didn't know how to command the heaviness and evil presence that I sensed to go, in Jesus name, or how to anoint the property to be consecrated as a dwelling place of the Lord.

I fell asleep lying on my right side curled up in a fetal position with my hands curled up under my face. This position gave me a sense of comfort. A few hours later, I awoke so petrified I was gasping for air. I couldn't breathe, my back was pinned on the bed, my legs were straight and tight, and my arms were rigid along my side. My whole body felt paralyzed. An evil, dark presence three times bigger than my body hovered approximately three feet above me and I feared it was going to fall and smother me. My heart raced as I attempted to move away. No muscles responded. I couldn't move!

Suddenly a force from within broke through and I heard, "Go, in the name of Jesus." To my amazement, it came out of my mouth. It sounded out of this world, certainly not my own voice. Then I shouted, "Jesus, Jesus, Jesus, Jesus..." I was filled with authority and a divine power unknown to me broke the darkness. It abruptly disappeared. My body was drenched in sweat as I slowly got up. I sat on the side of the bed and broke into tears realizing the terrifying ordeal from which the Lord had just saved me, by His amazing grace.

That experience, and many others that followed, taught me to be prepared for the unexpected attacks and to prioritize worship and prayer. My spiritual weapons needed to be sharpened daily. Above all, I discovered that we can never solely depend on our training in spiritual warfare or be afraid because of our lack of it. We can depend on Christ, the Anointed One, to rescue us. The battle is His!

Our Thoughts

2 Corinthians 10:5-6 "… casting down arguments and every high thing that exalts itself against the knowledge of God, bringing every thought into captivity to the obedience of Christ."

Our weapons destroy fortresses or strongholds. The arguments are human reasonings and "every high thing" corresponds to what is prideful and self-centered. We use our authority in Christ to demolish what the enemy has firmly established.

Obedience to Christ must always be our target. Whatever quenches our obedience to Him must be exposed and overcome. Divine wisdom means knowing God's thoughts and His ways, which are much higher than ours.

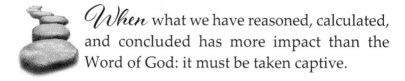 *When* what we have reasoned, calculated, and concluded has more impact than the Word of God: it must be taken captive.

Although we have the mind of Christ, our carnal mind has been exercised for so long it comes forth "naturally," and hinders the release of the supernatural. Therefore, we must now exercise the mind of Christ to war effectively.

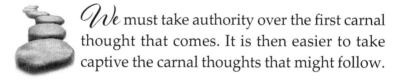 *We* must take authority over the first carnal thought that comes. It is then easier to take captive the carnal thoughts that might follow.

When we agree with the first carnal thought it leads to disobedience, multiplies the deception, and causes us to do the very thing we do not want to do. One thought leads to another, then another, and so on, until it becomes a fortified area. It is intended to get us to the point of acting out. We need to take authority over our carnal nature, and it needs to be brought low so that the higher thoughts and ways that come from Him are revealed.

We take ungodly thoughts captive by believing and speaking the Word of God. As we take authority over ungodly thoughts, we replace them with thoughts of obedience such as, "I can do all things through Christ, which strengthens me." As a result, our confession of faith grows, and obedience follows. It is a chain reaction.

Our adversary does everything he can to stop us from going forward. He is not threatened or concerned with our knowledge of the Word of God if we don't do anything with it.

 The moment we step out and become a doer of the Word, opposition increases.

We can't know about prayer if we don't pray. We can know we are to lay hands on the sick and they may recover, but if we don't lay hands on the sick, that knowledge does us no good. We may know we can command demons to flee, but if we don't do it, what good is that knowledge? As we go and grow *from glory to glory*, the Holy Spirit teaches us to take the necessary steps of faith.

When I began stepping out to minister, whether to someone in need of prayer or teaching or preaching on the radio, in a bible study or from a pulpit, I found myself warring in my mind around each assignment. The purpose of the battle, of course, was to cause me not to obey the leading of Lord.

Before I would speak, thoughts of inferiority, insecurity and condemnation would come from our adversary. These lies included: "you have not studied enough; you don't have any experience; people won't understand your French accent; others have taught on that before;" or, "you don't have time." The Holy Spirit began teaching me to overcome these thoughts with the truth of His leading: *I'm obeying the Lord; Greater is He who is in me than he who is in the world; the Lord will be the one speaking through my voice; I am led by the Lord and He anoints all that He appoints; or, I can do all things through Christ who strengthens me.* I would then receive peace and move forward trusting Him, and only Him!

During the assignment, satan would tempt me to look at what was happening in the room, someone asleep or another leaving the room. By faith, we take the steps and open our mouths. We learn to keep our eyes above, to disappear and yield to the flow of the Holy Spirit.

After completing God's assignments, a bombardment of lies would return: "you forgot to mention this or that; you didn't quote the right scripture; it was a failure, don't do it again; at least you tried, now go back to your accounting work, and so forth." These attacks came with a spirit of heaviness and I praise God for training me through it all to overcome the battles of the mind. I started to speak the truth out loud after every service. This prevented the lies from coming. The barrier the truth created protected my mind from listening to the lies. Instead, I would hear words of life in my spirit like: it's not what you say that ministers to people, *it's what the Holy Spirit makes them hear; my word always bears fruit; keep your focus on me and rest in my divine ability.*

There are times when the Holy Spirit will show us things we have said or done wrong. These instructions are only for us to know, to learn and be trained. It's not for us to go to others and say, "did you notice I used the wrong address for the scripture I just shared with you?" It's not for us to bring light upon our errors. The light shines upon what we need to know to improve our yielding to the Holy Spirit. The Holy Spirit uses correction but never uses condemnation. satan uses condemnation, and that's how we can detect the difference. God's voice lifts, edifies and encourages. The voice of the enemy brings us down and tries to stop us from speaking again while the voice of the Lord shows us how to do it better the next time.

What came to try to stop us from obeying the Lord is used as a stepping stone to do more in His name.

We are not to look at the fruits of our obedience for it may not be seen immediately at the time. 1 Corinthians 3:6 tells us: "I planted, Apollos watered, but God gave the increase." Signs and wonders follow the Word; we don't follow the signs and the wonders. We trust Him for the accomplishments. We trust that He moves, always. He touches, always. He blesses, always. We obey Him and trust the results are there whether we see them or not. The results are in His hands.

Can we count it all joy when we fall into diverse trials? Yes, when we understand what our Lord Jesus Christ achieved for us. It is one thing to walk through a trial, but another to endure it with joy. However, in doing so the fruit of the Spirit is seen as we continue to grow *from glory to glory.*

> **James 1:3-4** "… knowing that the testing of your faith produces patience. But let patience have its perfect work, that you may be perfect and complete, lacking nothing."

It is because we believe that we already have the victory in Him that we can count it all joy. The various trials help us achieve what we are called to do with more assurance and results. If we know to expect these attacks and to still rejoice while targeted by them, we will not be defeated when they come.

 When we say yes to the call, we can count on the enemy to fight back. Then our counting is not on the devil's winning, but on our victory. We do not fight for victory, but from a place of victory.

On the cross, the battle was won; that is why the fight is a good fight of faith.

We are to count it a matter of joy when our belief in the gospel is subject to various trials. It is a good thing for us to have the reality of our faith tested any way necessary. The longer it takes to receive what we have believed God for, the greater the victory.

> **Matthew 5:12** "Rejoice and be exceedingly glad, for great is your reward in heaven, for so persecuted they the prophets who were before you."

If we do not let patience have her perfect work but intervene on our own behalf, something might happen that prevents us from receiving the perfect work God has for us. His extension is for our expansion. When I think of joy, I think of Paul who took pleasure, meaning he jumped up and down with joy, in all that he endured. When Paul asked the Lord that his thorn in the flesh be removed, he heard and proclaimed the following:

2 Corinthians 12:9–10 "And He said to me, 'My grace is sufficient for you, for My strength is made perfect in weakness.' Therefore, most gladly I will rather boast in my infirmities, that the power of Christ may rest upon me. Therefore, I take pleasure in infirmities, in reproaches, in needs, in persecutions, in distresses, for Christ's sake. For when I am weak, then I am strong."

Let us never depend on our own strength, but when we have none, let us rejoice and count on His. The Greek word for strength is *dunamis,* which comes from the word *dunamai,* meaning to be able, or to have power. Its definition is a miraculous power and might. In our weakness, our ability comes forth because of Christ in us.

 When we feel the weakest, we are the strongest because we are in Him and He is in us. When we cannot, He can.

We take heed to this stepping stone while walking the others, not with fear but with faith. Christ is our great captain in this warfare. In His name the battle is waged, and by His power the victory is enforced! Christ in us is the hope of glory. The more we decrease, the more he increases! Praise Him forevermore!

Reflection

- What triumphs do you recall that came from unexpected trials?

- How did you handle the various trials that came with the adversity?

- What helps you keep your weapons sharpened?

- How do you war effectively against ungodly thoughts?

- Reflect on the last battle you were in. Evaluate your ability to count it all joy.

Action Steps

1 Review your daily routine, and if need be, change it to have more time in worship and prayer. Write down your decision.

2 Make a list of the battles that keep reoccurring and the victories you are believing to receive from the Lord.

3 Make a list of the scriptures you learned to stand on primarily to obey the leading of the Lord.

Prayer

Father,

Open my eyes to see what the battles are about in my life. Help me pray and worship daily to keep my weapons sharpened. Teach me to war effectively. Protect me from the fiery darts of the adversary. Lead and anoint me to do Your will. I yield myself to You to use me, and I trust You wholeheartedly. I take every thought captive to obey You, Lord. I rejoice in all circumstances knowing I belong to You and You turn all my trials into triumphs. Thank You, Father, in Jesus' name.

Amen.

CHAPTER 6

Acts 20: 24 *"But none of these things move me; nor do I count my life dear to myself, so that I may finish my race with joy, and the ministry which I received from the Lord Jesus, to testify to the gospel of the grace of God."*

DETERMINATION

As we seek and obey the leading of the Lord in His divine purpose, we find that to stay determined is an ESSENTIAL STEPPING STONE. To do so, remaining committed to the call of God despite all opposition takes preeminence. Discouragement, tiredness and constant battles come as an attempt to cause us to burn out and give up, thus walking away from the call.

God uses what the enemy brings our way to stir us up with increasing determination and passion.

Don't Fear

No matter what came his way, Paul remained faithful to the leading of the Lord. He said, "none of these things move me," and then, "nor do I count my life dear to myself." These two affirmations enabled him to move fearlessly and help us do so as well.

Paul said, "None of these things move me." What things? The bonds and afflictions he expected in every city. He was not moved by circumstances and made no account of them at all. He kept steadfast in the course laid before him. He remained immovable within himself at all times. Only God should move us out of the place He led us to, not trials and tribulations.

His expression of not counting his life dear unto himself reminds us of Christ who gave His life to redeem us. Are we prepared to serve God even if it means giving up our life? Not to count our life dear in the sense here indicated, is the only way to be able to stand firm in our calling. The word dear means costly, valuable. His life was not dearer to him than the Lord. It belonged to the Lord and was dear to Christ. In counting the cost of the call, laying down our life for the sake of the gospel must be considered and accepted. When we no longer fear to lose our life, we no longer fear in other areas as well.

In 1 Kings 19, when the Prophet Elijah heard that Jezebel wanted him to die, he believed it and ran for his life in fear. Then he wanted to die, the very thing he was escaping! Right before that he had won a battle against the prophets of Baal and conquered them. He had confidence in God and courageously turned his eyes upon the Lord and obeyed the assignment. He could conquer around 500 prophets of Baal when he focused on God, but only one woman's threat, "you are going to die," caused him to pay attention to himself and accept defeat. The moment he placed his eyes on himself, fear, death, depression, and oppression overwhelmed him.

We look to Jesus with every step we take. The moment we do so, we look away from ourselves and others. Our focus on Him enables us to stand by faith.

Fear of the future dissipates when our faith abides in Him.

During a mission trip, I started trembling from fever and excruciating pain all over my body. It felt like all my joints, muscles and organs were attacked by some mysterious ailment. The unknown cause made things worse. Calling a nurse, searching online for medical advice, or going to a hospital wasn't feasible. What's happening? After praying against anything that was not of God, I rested in the caring hands of our Lord Jesus. I beheld Him and recited the Word of God in my heart even though I couldn't speak it out loud. My attention stayed upon Him and it helped me press through the ordeal and trust the outcome. The schedule called for me to minister in the morning, in the afternoon and in the evening. The moment I stood on the platform, the Holy Spirit took over my frail body and ministered to the people. In amazement, I watched Him heal many people. Following each session, I would lie down exhausted, *Yes Lord, you are my healer*. I trust You. After three days, I remember praying, *Lord, thank you. If this is my time to go home to*

You, I rejoice that it is while serving You on a mission trip, glorifying Your name. Within a few minutes, the fever broke, and the pain was gone. I knew then that I could follow my journey led by the Holy Spirit, with no fear of death, no fear of the unknown, and no fear of trials and tribulations.

In my youth, fear accompanied me everywhere because of many extreme hardships and traumatic experiences. After I became a new creation in Christ, the Lord filled me with faith to the other extreme. Fear aims to stop us but is rendered powerless as we obey God.

Fear, not just of physical death but of the death of a relationship, a career, finances, a specific ministry, and so forth, including the fear of man, tries to hinder us from walking by faith and obeying the will of God. Fear also attempts to move us away from what we possess in Christ. It comes to quench our faith.

1 John 4:17-18 "Love has been perfected among us in this: that we may have boldness in the day of judgment; because as He is, so are we in this world. There is no fear in love; but perfect love casts out fear because fear involves torment. But he who fears has not been made perfect in love."

Perfect love casts out all fear. Love conquers fear. When fear seeks to grip me, in addition to some Psalms, I read First John because love, above all, is its main message.

 The more we feed our faith with the revelation of His love, the more we receive it and are perfected in it.

The opposite proves itself true: the more we feed our fears with the lies of the enemy, the more it grows and make us begin to question God's love. The instant we remember the reality of God's love, we began to experience peace, comfort, and safety.

 It is our growth into the image of Christ, not the growth of a building or a ministry that matters the most.

When that is our focus, we can let go of everything and move into the new as He leads us.

The Lord called me to the ministry one early morning in the spring of 1994 during my time of devotion while I was reading:

2 Corinthians 3:18 "But we all, with unveiled face, beholding as in a mirror the glory of the Lord, are being transformed into the same image from glory to glory, just as by the Spirit of the Lord."

The presence of the Lord permeated my bedroom and "from glory to glory" seemed to jump off the page. It felt like an electric current touched my entire body. During the following hour, the Lord expounded on the clarity of its meaning and resolved many of my questions about the Christ-like walk, and the purposes of God. Then a strong pull to go to the next chapter, first verse, drew me:

2 Corinthians 4:1 "Therefore, since we have this ministry, as we have received mercy, we do not lose heart."

I recall weeping from this encounter. Instead of the "we," I perceived "you" have this ministry, *"from glory to glory".* It came with the faith to step out into whatever lay ahead and a fearlessness only possible through Christ. Even before that happening, I would respond, *"from glory to glory"* to "how are you doing," or "what are you doing." Now with this unveiling, my entire being filled with worship and gratitude. To help myself and others in the *"glory to glory"* growth in Christ became my aim, by His grace.

My involvement in the church I attended included various ministries, so I thought the Lord would lead me to do one of them in a different capacity. Instead, He led me to start a radio program called "Glory to Glory," mentioned in an earlier chapter, and to start, "From Glory to Glory Ministries." It evolved into a monthly evangelistic meeting, then weekly meetings, and eventually the establishment of a Church. During each phase, the Lord gave specific instructions and confirmed the going and growing *from glory to glory.*

Knowing we go and grow *from glory to glory* encourages us in our journey. Fear, disappointments, and discouragement can cause us to lose heart. By the grace of God, we keep fighting the good fight of faith, trusting He will help us finish the race.

Philippians 1:6 "being confident of this very thing, that He who has begun a good work in you will complete it until the day of Jesus Christ."

Don't Let Your Guard Down

We set healthy boundaries to guard our hearts and walk in transformation with steadfastness and determination. These keep out encumbrances and helps us stand in our divine identity. Boundaries form a dividing line, protect our privacy and signal no trespassing to possible intruders.

The process of establishing and strengthening our borders unfolds over time. We discover our value and the value of others in Christ, thereby learning to respect one another.

 *We* cannot respect what we don't value.

We honor others as we recognize and accept their boundaries as well as our own.

As a minister, we learn to seek the Lord before taking on a responsibility to confirm it is His will. We might not be the one He will use to meet that need, and if we are not, our input might be an interference. He leads us with inward peace.

 The restraints and constraints of the Holy Spirit often cannot be understood, only followed.

In our personal lives, we define our priorities and pursue our assignments to maintain them within our sphere of influence. Our relationship with God is foremost, then our spouse, our children, our careers, and our volunteering in a church or ministry. When we say no to what hinders this order of priorities, we make room for more of what the Lord has for us.

We run this Christian race as we remain on the tracks, focus on the finish line and what lays ahead trusting the second wind He graciously releases along the way. Boundaries that are often overlooked are usually the ones formed through our sight, hearing and speech. To insure we don't waver from our divine purpose and stay focused, we must guard what we see, hear and speak in the natural— and sharpen our spiritual senses.

1. Our eyes

What we behold determines our outlook and perspective.

 *What* we dwell on,
eventually we dwell in.

Those things we see in the natural affect our thoughts and can cloud our decisions. Television programs or movies we watch must be carefully selected.

What God has done can only be seen through spiritual eyes. Faith is the evidence of things not seen. While we are waiting for the manifestation of what we believe God will do, we need to spend time with the Lord so our vision remains clear and sharply focused. Faith sees what cannot be seen with natural eyes.

2 Corinthians 5:7 "For we walk by faith, not by sight."

As we seek God for direction, He anoints our eyes to see some of His answers ahead of time. When we see them, we speak them forth with confidence. By faith, we proclaim the truth and see the lies being rebuked instantly. The more we believe the promises of God in our hearts, the more we can declare them to the darkness that occupies our surroundings.

2. Our ears

We stand on what the Word of God says, regardless of any other word our natural ears might hear. We should close them to negative words. This includes the doubts, unbelief and criticism that comes through others. Our ears are not to be used as garbage cans. It is essential when we hear someone begin to tear down another, instead of building them up, to stop that person, in love, or remove ourselves from the situation as quickly as possible.

> **Romans 10:17** " So then faith comes by hearing, and hearing by the word of God."

Fear comes by hearing, and hearing by the word of satan. When we feel oppressed, fearful and defeated it is not of God.

 We recognize faith vs. fear by detecting flesh vs. Spirit.

Anything that comes to elevate anyone is not of God. We must guard against words that tell us we will be famous or called to the nations! Of course, personal prophecy will relate to us and will say things about us, but the focus will be about who the Lord is and what He will do in and through us.

 It's never about how great we are, but always how great God is.

Does what we hear identify with "self," or "Him"? It is important to identify who is being exalted. The enemy, satan, comes to lift flesh and feed the ego of man. The Holy Spirit always comes to lift Jesus! When the Lord is being glorified, we grow in faith and grace and are lifted to a place of worshipping Him! More of Him is the fruit that we look for in every situation.

3. Our mouths

God will show us what to share and what to keep quiet. We use caution while sharing with others. The taming of our tongue is tested with every step we take.

We place a guard over our mouth understanding that life and death are in the power of the tongue. We pray the Lord enables us to tame our tongue, so our words may edify and minister grace unto the hearers. Words spoken by the flesh, out of anger, hurt those they are spoken *to* as well as the one spoken **through.**

> **Psalms 141:3** "Set a guard, O Lord, over my mouth; Keep watch over the door of my lips."

When we say things we shouldn't say, the sword of the Spirit, the Word of God, is hindered from flowing freely. We are called to speak forth the truth of God's word with authority and power. We must beware of the ways we can be pulled into other people's conversations. Gossip is very destructive. Sometimes our silence is taken as our agreement with what is said. It is best to move away from a conversation that is improper. So much assumption is made by others when things are said that misrepresent the truth. Talebearers spread rumors and lies causing a lot of hurt in the Body of Christ.

We cannot answer for others but can pray for our own mouth to be controlled by the power of the Holy Spirit. As led by the Lord, our silence in response to opposition brings about a peaceful rest in Him. We can condemn every word that comes against us in judgment. This includes what is known and unknown, as well as words we spoke.

> **Isaiah 54:17** "No weapon formed against you shall prosper, And every tongue which rises against you in judgment You shall condemn. This is the heritage of the servants of the LORD, And their righteousness *is* from Me," Says the LORD."

We endeavor to keep these openings naturally shut and spiritually attuned. As we do, our eyes, ears, and mouths increase in anointing for the service of the Lord.

The boundaries we set in place cannot be trusted apart from the boundaries God sets on our behalf. He protects us from ourselves. He secures our borders, even in our unawareness of the need. We might feel restricted when, in fact, we are protected. He tears down borders we think are firm so He can enlarge our territory.

For our protection, some relationships come to a halt;

others remain when we wish they wouldn't. A door closes to a potential job while another we didn't want keeps coming around. A loan application gets rejected. The house we wanted to purchase goes to another buyer. The fences the Lord builds around us hinder unseen enemies from making inroads into our lives. We can rely on Him when our adversary attacks our borders in unidentified ways.

 Insignificant encounters can become relevant opportunities.

As we look back on our lives, we praise God for making peace within our borders when we needed His help.

We all matter to the Lord. Regardless of the measures we take in the natural to secure our safety, only the boundaries God establishes for us remain stable and impenetrable. We belong to Him and He watches over His property. He works all things together for the good. We find God is our shield and strong defense.

> **Romans 8:28** "And we know that all things work together for good to those who love God, to those who are the called according to His purpose."

We can serve the Lord and stand against all pressure to bow down to the enemy's ways because we belong to our God and have been delivered from the hands of the kingdom of darkness.

When all we see is the Lord, we can walk with His peace guarding our hearts and minds.

Though we walk in the shadow of death, we fear no evil because God is with us. The enemy looks at the way we walk through the fire, and when he sees that the Lord is with us, he knows he cannot win. He knows he has lost, and the Lord is watching over us.

Don't Give Up

In our service to the Lord, we learn by His grace to be steadfast and immovable. Fixity (the quality or state of being fixed; stability; permanence) of purpose, boldness, tenacity, courage, fearlessness, valor, vigor, stamina, and perseverance are necessary. We sharpen these character traits by not giving up.

Our adversary, satan, often tempts us to give up. He lies to many about who they really are to prevent them from doing what they are called to do. Paul is expressing that no matter what awaits him, he is prepared for anything. He could not be moved from the hope of the gospel, the ministry of the Word, or his journey. His faith could not be shaken; fear could not enter him; nothing could abort his purpose. Nothing, not even the possibility of death, could move him away from following the leading of the Lord.

Prior to this he said:

> **Acts 20:22-23**, "And see, now I go bound in the spirit to Jerusalem, not knowing the things that will happen to me there, except that the Holy Spirit testifies in every city, saying that chains and tribulations await me."

Paul was bound in the Spirit to go to Jerusalem. Our unity to what the Holy Spirit leads us to do will keep us anchored to His purpose.

 To the degree that we are bound in the Spirit, we can say no to what is contrary to His purpose and tries to tie us down.

We are bound in the Spirit when we are so compelled to do something that no one can stop us, regardless of the outside circumstances. With surety in our steps, we become fearless and move with holy boldness.

 We recognize our call to action by our inability to get away from it, no matter how much we try.

The more we attempt to do something else, the more the leading to do that one thing grows. In other words, we cannot get away from the call; it keeps knocking at our door.

Paul knew by the Spirit of God that he would experience restrictions, but the bonds he had with the Lord were stronger.

He was so bound to the Spirit that bonds and afflictions that tried to deter him could not hold him.

He was firm and unwavering.

When we are bound to the covenant, bound to the spiritual realm, bound to His easy yoke, bound to Him through the scarlet thread of His blood— no other bonds can tie us down. The unacceptable bonds will get disconnected one by one. We cannot be unequally yoked. That would hinder the call, quench the Holy Spirit and move us away from finishing our course. Our relationships will be sifted one after the other. God knows our hidden weaknesses and protects us by cutting ties in our lives that cannot remain if we are to move forward.

To be determined is to be fully persuaded.

Hebrews 11:17-19 "By faith Abraham, when he was tested, offered up Isaac, and he who had received the promises offered up his only begotten son, of whom it was said, *'In Isaac your seed shall be called,'* concluding that God was able to raise *him* up, even from the dead, from which he also received him in a figurative sense."

Abraham was counting on the fact that God could raise Isaac from the dead. He believed God's promise that he was going to be the father of many nations. That was the only outcome he could foresee. His only conclusion was that a resurrection would occur. Counting on that eventually helped him go through what he was facing. He was so sure about it that he was ready to offer up Isaac. We can say that we are ready to do whatever is asked of us, but to walk in it is another matter altogether. Even Peter said he would not deny the Lord, and yet he did.

Abraham looked ahead to the promise and did not look at the circumstances. He got up early to obey quickly and told his servants to stay at the bottom of the mountain, that he and the lad were going up to worship and would be coming back. In doing so, he was confessing the outcome of the situation. Their coming through was not an issue to him.

He didn't know the exact place to climb to, just the area. It's after he proceeded to follow God's leading that more specifics were revealed to him. He continued to keep his ears open to new instructions and therefore could hear the angel tell him to stop when it was time. We don't give up obeying God trusting the steps He leads in the process. It's not a stubborn attitude to not give up on this thing or that thing, but it is knowing God will do what only He can do! Abraham focused on what God could do instead of what "he" could do. We must believe in the resurrection to walk in its power.

Regardless of the directives or circumstances, we can determine to keep on keeping on.

I faced personal situations in which the Lord helped me remain determined and reassured me not to give up. The most memorable situation happened during the last year of the School of Ministry I attended. Both my daughters were still living at home. I had moved from a full time receptionist/bookkeeping job to part time to start my own bookkeeping agency, so I could pursue my education.

One evening, as I was falling asleep, my oldest daughter walked in the bedroom appearing troubled and said, "Mom, what does it mean when your breasts hurt?" I jumped off the bed and replied, ""Oh my God, you are pregnant!!!" I reached out to her, embraced her and we began processing the implications of this unexpected news. She attended college and was unmarried.

Only three months later, I walked towards the room of my youngest daughter one evening after work, knocked at the door and heard, "Mom, I have something to tell you! It's terrible!" I went in, sat by her bedside and said, what is it my love? What could be so terrible? You are here, alive! Surely that is what matters the most! She replied, "I'm pregnant." It was her senior year in high school.

Leaving the school of ministry and looking for extra work to cover the costs of caring for two daughters, and two soon to be born grandchildren, appeared to be the most feasible option. However, in my spirit it made no logical sense with what the Lord had placed on my heart. After fasting and praying, the call to continue the ministry training was reaffirmed and with deep-seated conviction, I resolved to follow the Lord. With that assurance, I knew He would take care of the needs as I sought Him faithfully.

After my resolve, He opened a door to do the accounting for a company that would pay more for part time than I used to make full time, and enough to continue the school and care for my household.

It is through our determination that we will abound in the work of the Lord. Not much will be accomplished if we are not steadfast. Endurance and determination must overcome any desire to quit.

I Corinthians 15: 58 "Therefore, my beloved brethren, be steadfast, immovable, always abounding in the work of the Lord, knowing that your labor is not in vain in the Lord."

 Unmovable, unbothered, unaffected, unshakable, bound to be determined— we are Ambassadors of Christ.

Reflection

- How did you overcome a fearful situation?

- What helps you set and keep healthy boundaries?

- How do you develop determination to walk in His purpose?

- What lies has the enemy used against you in his attempt to prevent you from doing what you are called to do?

- What helped you when you were tempted to give up?

Action Steps

1 Make a list identifying the things you might see, hear or say that you need to guard against.

2 Make a list of what you keep doing, or not doing, to keep healthy boundaries in place.

3 List some bonds that have been disconnected from you. What were the results?

Prayer

Father,

Help me stay free from fear, except for the reverent fear I have for You. By Your grace, show me the boundaries I should set in place with more surety. Thank You for protecting me from the unknown. I consecrate my eyes, ears and voice to You. Anoint them for Your glory. Give me the ability to persevere regardless of what comes my way. Lead me with surety in my steps. You never give up on me and I will not give up obeying You, regardless of the cost. I am so blessed, always! I give You praise, honor and glory! In Jesus' name.

Amen.

CHAPTER 7

1st Timothy 1:12 *"And I thank Christ Jesus our Lord who has enabled me, because He counted me faithful, putting me into the ministry."*

DIVINE ENDOWMENT

The stepping stones we learned in the previous chapters lead us to a level of faithfulness to God that cannot be shaken. It results in an abounding anointing for ministry. We have considered what we should count on to answer our divine calling. This last chapter reflects on what God counts on, and how it relates to the STEPPING STONE WE NEED THE MOST— divine endowment, the empowerment to do whatever He calls us to be and do for His glory.

Priority

What does God count on? Our faithfulness.

Paul was faithful because he believed in the reality of the Lord. This was a result of his dramatic conversion on the road to Damascus. He was on his way to arrest those who had faith in the Lord when he was, himself, arrested by the Lord. This encounter was such that he asked the Lord, "What do you want me to do?" From that point on he surrendered and sought to do the will of God.

We clearly see in our scripture the connection between being faithful and being enabled. The word *enabled* comes from the Greek word *endunamoo*, which means "to empower." One of the root words is *dunamis*, which describes a force or a miraculous power. In other words, it is not just being able to do something, but being empowered to accomplish it as He would by the word of the Lord, "not by might, nor by power but by My spirit." (Zechariah 4:6)" This power is the manifestation of the Holy Spirit through us to do what we cannot do on our own.

Faithfulness is a necessary qualification for the ministry. We are made faithful and kept so by the grace of our Lord Jesus Christ. We are stewards of the manifold grace and mysteries of God. The more we realize this and receive all that comes from Him, the more we cherish whatever He places in our hands to accomplish. His faithfulness expands ours. We should be so grateful and humbled by His glory!

 As we are faithful with what He gives us to do, He multiplies it. We must be good stewards of what God gives us, no matter how insignificant it appears to be.

Paul continued his tent-making profession while he obeyed the Lord's direction and instruction. It's essential to know that the Lord can call upon us no matter where we are. Elisha was plowing, Moses was tending sheep, and the disciples had careers when they were apprehended for a specific purpose. Our Lord Jesus, Himself, was occupied as a carpenter. We do not have to stop what we are doing to fulfill our purpose; we just need to be faithful where we are planted. The Lord will use whatever place or occupation we find ourselves in to fulfill His purpose. Many anointed believers are being used by God in the market place releasing His glory!

While working in an accounting position for a printing company, I was led to start the radio program which then expanded to evangelistic meetings on Thursday nights. This schedule required leaving work at 5:00 pm, a rush home to shower, and arriving early to set up the room to prepare for the gathering at 7:00 pm. With joy I kept this monthly, then weekly assignment. As a volunteer at the church I attended, I was thankful for whatever opportunity became available. It was a joy loving the Lord and serving others in any capacity.

I continued to work in the accounting field for ten years while I founded and pastored the church. Shortly after my daughters moved out and my lease expired, I moved to a room on the top floor where the church services were being held. The sanctuary was my living room. By His grace, I waited for His timing to stop working at my job. When I would go to work, I would look at it as another place to minister and prayed for His help to remain faithful.

The Holy spirit knows where we are. Our faithfulness transpires in our daily fellowship with Him. We prioritize our time in the word and in worship. We commune with The Lord and as we enjoy His presence, He leads us to minister when we least expect it. Ministry might include a gentle touch, a prayer, sharing a scripture, even a word of exhortation to people we encounter. It could be a stranger in a grocery store, another worshipper at the church, or a co-worker we never spoke to before. We minister to one as we would to hundreds, with a grateful heart.

No assignment appears too small when we serve such a big God!

We stay available to Him and trust His leading. Even with no clear mission in sight, we remain faithful, content in Him.

Matthew 25:21 "His lord said to him, 'Well done, good and faithful servant; you were faithful over a few things, I will make you ruler over many things. Enter into the joy of your lord.'"

When God opens a door of opportunity, we can trust His ability will manifest because of our availability.

How can we serve Him without His empowerment? Apart from it, we find ourselves unable to obey Him. We can trust that our Lord Jesus, The Anointed One, desires and delights in outpouring this divine endowment upon every member of His body, that He may be glorified. Our part is to believe, receive and yield wholeheartedly!

Our involvement in co-laboring with Him is to yield.

We help Him by not helping Him.

We surrender to His working, knowing that apart from Him we really can do nothing; but because we are a part of Him— and with Him all things are possible. The more we grow in Christ, the more 2 Corinthians 3:5 becomes a reality: "Not that we are sufficient of ourselves to think anything as of ourselves; but our sufficiency is of God."

As we connect being faithful and being enabled, we can proclaim in agreement with the following:

> **Ephesians 3:20–21** "Now unto him that is able to do exceeding abundantly above all that we ask or think, according to the power that worketh in us, Unto him be glory in the church by Christ Jesus throughout all ages, world without end. Amen."

To trust the Lord despite ourselves and keep our eyes on who He is in and through us, rather than who we are in our flesh, are the main keys to our becoming trustworthy. When asked to watch over something that is not ours, we are oftentimes more careful than we would be with our own possessions. What an honor to walk circumspectly, with caution, to honor Him!

When our attitude is to go the extra mile in every endeavor, we advance in our spiritual journey. What a privilege to be His servant! Our reverent fear of God must be greater than our fear of man. Our aim remains to please God, not others. To know that what the Lord entrusts us with is His, and not ours, takes our ambassadorship and stewardship to a new reality. We represent Him and walk in increased *accountability*. When we receive a promotion in our place of work, we also accept more responsibility. This also applies when engaged in the ministry.

The more that is given to us, the more that is required. What is given to us is sometimes not revealed until after what is required has been completed. Therefore, it is difficult to understand the why behind our circumstances as we move in faith and obedience. The more we give of what He has given us, the more we receive.

 With every increase comes a new level of authority which is accompanied with a corresponding anointing.

Power

When He introduced the Holy Spirit, the third person of the Trinity, our Lord told us that He would dwell *with* us and be *in* us.

> **John 14:16-17** "And I will pray the Father, and
> He will give you another Helper, that He may
> abide with you forever—the Spirit of truth,
> whom the world cannot receive, because it
> neither sees Him nor knows Him; but you
> know Him, for He dwells with you and will
> be in you."

The Holy Spirit would be sent to execute all that was purchased for us on Calvary, abiding with us forever and revealing Jesus, the Christ, to us. Before we were born again, the Holy Spirit was with us upon our conversion. He also dwells in us. His indwelling, the Holy Spirit's work of conversion, illumination, and regeneration, brings transformation in our lives. As we are transformed into the image of Christ, the Holy Spirit convicts instead of condemns, and comforts instead of crushes. He draws us closer to His purpose as He pulls us with gentleness and leads us always *from glory to glory*. Although His work is done on the inside, He proceeds to come upon us to enable work to be done on the outside.

In addition to being *with* us and *in* us, He also comes *upon* us. This infilling is referred to in the following scriptures:

> **Acts 1:8** "But you shall receive power when
> the Holy Spirit has come upon you; and you
> shall be witnesses to Me in Jerusalem, and in
> all Judea and Samaria, and to the end of the
> earth."

Luke 24:49 "Behold, I send the promise of my Father upon you: but tarry in the city of Jerusalem, until you are endued with power from on high."

The promise of this baptism of the Holy Spirit is for every believer. To be endued with this power from on high is like sinking into a garment, or to invest with clothing. When we put on Christ, we put off the old man. Christ is the Greek word Christos, meaning anointed; that is, the Messiah. Jesus Christ is the Anointed One, and through the Spirit of Christ in us, He operates as He wills.

 The Holy Spirit uses us; we do not use Him.

Indeed, we are the Body of Christ. It is Christ in us that is the hope of glory.

Paul tells us to be filled with the Spirit, not to be drunk with wine, using the comparison to describe being under the influence of the Holy Spirit and under His control. In addition to the initial baptism of the Holy Spirit which all believers can receive by faith, we should wholeheartedly seek to be continually filled. We do so through the laying on of hands and we keep ourselves edified by speaking in tongues.

Ephesians 5:18-21 "And do not be drunk with wine, in which is dissipation; but be filled with the Spirit, speaking to one another in psalms and hymns and spiritual songs, singing and making melody in your heart to the Lord, giving thanks always for all things to God the Father in the name of our Lord Jesus Christ, submitting to one another in the fear of God."

Jesus tells us to come to Him to drink, not to anyone else, and not to depend on man-made methods. We drink as we receive from Him, by faith, all that He is and has. We pray in tongues for edification, worship, and read the word. We spend time with Him and do not even realize the rivers are flowing.

 *We* are filled to be spilled.

John 7:37-39 "On the last day, that great day of the feast, Jesus stood and cried out, saying, 'If anyone thirsts, let him come to Me and drink. He who believes in Me, as the Scripture has said, out of his heart will flow rivers of living water.' But this He spoke concerning the Spirit, whom those believing in Him would receive; for the Holy Spirit was not yet given, because Jesus was not yet glorified."

During another encounter, they were not only filled with the Holy Spirit, but the place where they were assembled was shaken. The power of God is greater than a man's power to withstand Him!

Acts 4:29-31 "Now, Lord, look on their threats, and grant to Your servants that with all boldness they may speak Your word, by stretching out Your hand to heal, and that signs and wonders may be done through the name of Your holy Servant Jesus. And when they had prayed, the place where they were assembled together was shaken; and they were all filled with the Holy Spirit, and they spoke the word of God with boldness."

I experienced various encounters with God. They confirmed His directions, took me to a deeper place of worship, increased my desire to seek and obey His will and fueled the fire of the Holy Spirit upon my life. These encounters remain vivid to this day because of their impact.

One of them took place during a prayer meeting with just two other people present. After praying corporately, we began praying individually, resting in the presence of God. After approximately thirty minutes, I sensed oil being poured out on me and dripping down the sides of my face. With it came a covering of love and peace. My hands and my head shook from such a tangible presence of His glory. It stopped after around fifteen minutes just as quickly as it started. I got up to look for a towel and asked the others, "did you pour out oil on me?" They said, "no, we don't have any." I went to the bathrooms and heard, I have anointed you. It took me some time to wash because I didn't want to remove the oil! The Lord showed me that He wanted me to know that He, Himself, anointed me and to walk with confidence in Him, *from glory to glory!*

Another encounter happened while attending a bible study on our spiritual authority. It was on a weekday evening, and only 11 people were registered. The rest of the church was very quiet as no other activities were in progress. On my way to the restrooms, I noticed the hallways were empty. All the other students remained in the classroom. It was easy to notice who was there, in and out of the class. On my way back to the room this lady moved toward me. She was a beautiful African American woman with mid- length hair, striking shiny eyes, no makeup, dressed very simply in a long skirt with a roomy, flowy blouse. I had never seen her before.

She approached me indicating she wanted to ask me something. I thought maybe directions. She intently looked at me and said, "Our Lord Jesus told me to impart His fire to you." I looked in her hands and didn't see anything. She extended her hand gesturing for me to give her my hand. She then placed one index finger in the palm of my right hand. Fire went inside of me, from the top of my head to the sole of my feet. I was filled with the fire of God. I closed my eyes from the heaviness of the glory. When I opened them, she was gone. I never saw her again.

I stood there for a few minutes trying to collect myself. What had just happened? Could I walk? Where is the room of the class I'm attending? I felt as though I was in some cloud; some supernatural place. I walked back into the room as in a daze. I sat down, and tears started running down my cheeks. I can't remember what was said the rest of the class, which was about another twenty minutes. All I could feel was this shaking going on inside my body. The Lord sent someone, could have been an angel, to impart a touch of the fire of the Holy Spirit on me! How wonderful is our Lord!

Purpose

The purpose of the anointing is to preach the gospel to the poor, to heal the brokenhearted, to preach deliverance to the captives, and recovering of sight to the blind, and to set at liberty them that are bruised.

Luke 4:18-19 "THE SPIRIT OF THE LORD IS UPON ME, BECAUSE HE HAS ANOINTED ME TO PREACH THE GOSPEL TO THE POOR; HE HAS SENT ME TO HEAL THE BROKENHEARTED, TO PROCLAIM LIBERTY TO THE CAPTIVES AND RECOVERY OF SIGHT TO THE BLIND, TO SET AT LIBERTY THOSE WHO ARE OPPRESSED; TO PROCLAIM THE ACCEPTABLE YEAR OF THE LORD."

The *anointing* can be defined as the manifestation of the power of the Holy Spirit in our lives. This anointing *upon* us is for service. It is *to do.*

Whatever we are called to do, in every place, relates to this scripture. We do so through the demonstration of the reality of Christ in our lives, and as we become doers of the Word of God.

 We do not seek after a title, but after a function. We can trust the unction for the function, not for a title.

Some can have a title but not operate in what the title represents. When we simply seek to share Christ through our lives, in every place, His anointing comes upon us to touch others. It works in everything that we do, including our daily tasks. It's a stamp to the world around us that the Lord is with us. The power of God is for *His* purpose. It is the *power of God,* not ours.

As God opens doors for us, all we can do is walk

through them, by faith. We are not to walk by sight. The empowerment will come when it is needed, not a second before. Again, the Holy Spirit uses us; we do not use Him.

2 Corinthians 4:7 "But we have this treasure in earthen vessels, that the excellence of the power may be of God and not of us."

The third encounter happened during a visit I made to the Brownsville revival. I was a little skeptical about some manifestations I had heard happened there: people falling on the floor, shaking, weeping, laughing, and more. The first night I stayed in the balcony watching, wondering, and praying. At first, I could hear myself being critical because of its unfamiliarity. That night when I went back to my room I repented and told the Lord that I wanted all that He had for me, and He could touch me however He wanted.

The next day I attended the service on the main floor. At the end of it, a young man, a teenager around fifteen years old, approached me and said, "Can I pray for you?" I looked to make sure he had a badge confirming he was part of the prayer team. I said, "sure." He gently placed his right hand on my forehead and said, "more of Jesus."

The power of God came upon me so strong that I couldn't stand under it. I fell under its impact and remained there for a long time. An overwhelming sense of the presence of the Lord overshadowed me. His love, comfort and joy flooded my soul. At that moment, Lindell Cooley and the worship team were playing a tune with Luke 4:18-19. After they ended the song, it continued for me. I kept hearing it except it was like a personal message to me from the Lord, "The Spirit of the Lord has anointed *you* to preach the gospel to the poor, to heal the broken hearted, to proclaim liberty to the captives and recovery of sight to the blind, to set at liberty those who are oppressed." This lasted until the place closed and someone touched me, saying, "It's time to go home."

The following days all I could do was weep. I was being emptied of hurt, pain, fear, and so much more, and filled with an abundance of the life of Christ. My visit there came about as a part of the celebration of my graduation from the School of Ministry. This experience not only reaffirmed the calling but confirmed that the anointing of the Lord would be there to help me with any assignment. Most of all, the Lord released a fresh infilling upon me, so

I could be "filled to be spilled." I had received many fillings but none like this specific outpouring for the purpose He had placed ahead of me.

The encounters I experienced with the move of the Holy Spirit were used by God to prepare me as a vessel in His hands. Each time He touched me, He removed things in me that were in His way. Let's surrender to His ways, no matter what they are, and be careful not to refuse what might be of Him. Oh, that we would not grieve, quench or resist the Holy Spirit!

 We often only understand our lives by looking backward.

This scripture becomes so significant:

1 Thessalonians 5:24 "He who calls you is faithful, who also will do it."

Knowing *He* is faithful, helps us remain faithful and trust Him to work in and through us as He wills.

 Our part in co-laboring with Him is to yield and obey.

We help Him by not helping Him. Our tendency is to question, "What should I do"? It's really about what *He*

does, not us. We might never know what that is. We do our part in obedience. We never know how far reaching something we do today will be.

 Every joint supply, and only God gives the increase.

1 Corinthians 3:7 "So then neither he who plants is anything, nor he who waters, but God who gives the increase."

Our ministry is to the Lord first. We worship *Him*, fellowship with *Him,* seek *His* will, *His* ways and *His* Word above all. We retain an awareness of His presence and acknowledge Him in all our ways. When we minister to others, whether one-on-one or to a group, we do so from our heart and rely on what the Holy Spirit would have them hear. He is the one who teaches them.

We are the vessels of the Lord Jesus. He is the head.

 Our mouths, hands and feet are His and can only be so when our hearts are His!

Christ comes over us to work through us and overpowers us to say and do what we cannot on our own. It's supernatural; the anointing for our calling!

Reflection

- What helped you remain faithful?

- What opposition did you overcome that came to move you out of the place where God called you?

- How did you notice in your own life the relationship between being faithful and walking into what God called you to do?

- Recall an encounter you had with the Lord. What resulted from it?

- How did you learn to be still while having a zeal to be used by God?

Action Steps

1 Pray for a fresh infilling of the Holy Spirit.

2 Make a list of what you have seen and are seeing the Lord do through you.

3 List what you noticed helped or hindered the flow of the anointing on your life. Pray for God's guidance on what to do accordingly.

Prayer

Father,

Help me to remain faithful to You in every situation. I desire Your will to be done. I yield myself to You and will obey You, by Your grace. Thank You for opening doors in Your timing. I'm grateful for all You have done and are doing in and through me. I trust You to give the increase. Oh, that I may walk by faith and not by sight! I thirst after You. More of You, Jesus, less of me.

Anoint me for Your glory, I pray, in Jesus' name.

Amen.

CONCLUSION

I trust the Lord has ministered to you through this book. In your journey, if you find a battle in any of these steps, ask the Lord to show you which one to reaffirm.

When you face trials, rededicate yourself, remain determined and trust His divine endowment. You will go through these bits of wisdom again and again.

Every time you go through this book, the Holy Spirit will bring light in different areas based on your walk at the time. I believe you will bring forth fruit that will remain, and whatever you ask of the Father in the name of Jesus, He may give it to you, as we read in:

> **John 15:16** "You have not chosen Me, but I chose you and appointed you, that you should go and bring forth fruit, and *that* your fruit should remain: that whatever you ask the Father in My name, He may give you."

Never pay attention to satan's lies when they come against you. You are in Christ and Christ is in you. Giving in to these lies leads to thoughts of giving up. Keep on looking unto Jesus, the author and the finisher of your faith.

As He has released confirmation, instruction, and revelation to you, remember that He will bestow upon you the anointing for the calling; the unction for every function.

I exhort you to finish the race knowing your reward comes from Him. As you make room for Him, the gift makes room for you. Proverbs 18:16 "A man's gift makes room for him, And brings him before great men". Go forth in the name of Jesus! "Not by might, nor by power, but by the Spirit," says the Lord. Fight the good fight of faith! You are a winner, victorious in Christ! Mighty warrior go forward no matter the cost and do whatever it takes!

The good works that have been ordained for us are the result of His workings. As with a beautiful fabric, He connects each thread for the establishing of His kingdom. I give God praise, honor, and glory for joining us through these words and much more that we will one day see.

> **Ephesians 2:10** "For we are his workmanship, created in Christ Jesus unto good works, which God prepared beforehand that we should walk in them."

What a joy to be a bondservant of Christ! In counting the cost, it was all worth it. Above all, we give our all for His all indeed. We continue to go *from glory to glory*, from faith to faith, from strength to strength.

We can proclaim, "In His hands I rest. In His care I stand. In His Word I abide. In His love I remain. In His glory I glory. In Him I live and move and have my being."

My prayer for you is this

2 Thessalonians 1:11-12 "Wherefore also we pray always for you that our God would count you worthy of this calling, and fulfill all the good pleasure of His goodness, and the work of faith with power, that the name of our Lord Jesus Christ may be glorified in you, and you in him, according to the grace of our God and the Lord Jesus Christ."

Amen

REFERENCES

Strong, James. *Strong's Hebrew and Greek Dictionary.* (From Rick Meyers' e-sword.net)

Vine, W. E. *Vine's Expository Dictionary of Biblical Words.* (Nashville: Thomas Nelson, Inc., 1985), 283

Webster, Noah. *Noah Webster's Dictionary of American English,* 1828 Facsimile Edition. (Foundation for American Christian Education, 1967)

NUGGETS OF TRUTH

Chapter 1

- There cannot be a resurrection if there is no crucifixion.

- Our identification in Christ gives us access to new realms of the reality of His glory.

- Trying so hard to do so in our own strength often binds us even more because we focus on the problem more than the solution.

- The cross represents the crossroad where the flesh and the spirit intersect.

- By faith, we appropriate all the Lord has accomplished on the cross.

- We conquer the power of our weaknesses, empowered by the Spirit of Christ.

- How could I answer His call if I answered my flesh above His will for my life?

- To trust God for what He can do, we must meditate on who He is and as we grasp His character, we rely on His ability. It's to the same degree we know the Lord that we can trust Him.

- To answer the call of God, we need to turn over to Him that divine call, so He can accomplish it in and through us without our flesh getting in the way.

- The trust in ourselves decreases as our trust in God increases.

- When Christ becomes our motive for ministry, doors open for Him, not for us.

- Our desire to obey Him outweighs our fears.

- In Christ, we can best help others by remaining in our place of victory and being an example, so they can also take that step of faith.

- When you know you have died to the flesh, and live in the spirit in Christ, you can tell satan, "you can't kill me, I'm already dead."

- After we have tried things our own way and are ready to allow Him to have His way, He then leads the way.

Chapter 2

- We cannot ascertain how to reach a future position without first assessing our current one.

- We must forsake all for the sake of the call.

- When we, and all we have belong to the Lord, we do not have to worry about how to keep it.

- To expect the unexpected helps us grow in awareness and not be moved.

- Never stop starting.

- As we seek a heart knowledge, we learn to go through things in life because of who we know, not what we know.

- What we do portrays a greater message than what we say.

- We must say no to the former to say yes to the new.

- It's not only what we say, but what the Holy Spirit enables others to hear.

- When we start walking in the newness of life, we realize what was can no longer be.

- His love can flow more freely in and through us to others when they can no longer dictate our oneness with Him.

- We cannot seek God's approval and man's approval at the same time.
- We cannot expect from others what only God can give.
- Humility is the gateway to knowing Him.
- Humility enables us to overcome offenses and focus on our own transformation.

Chapter 3

- The more we are set apart for Him, the more God shows us what He has set apart for us.

- Anything that hinders us from the excellency of the knowledge of Christ is worth losing.

- Dedicating ourselves pertains to not just our surrendering our lives to the Lord but doing so with our actions.

- The Holy Spirit reveals to heal.

- We move forward when we recognize the areas where we have progressed.

- Whatever gifts of the Holy Spirit flow through us, if we are without love, they are rendered ineffective.

- The fruit of the Holy Spirit comes before the gifts.

- Integrity will meet a prosperity that will last for eternity.

- Success in appearance only, not birthed from integrity of heart, falls to nothing.

- What is on the inside comes out under pressure.

- The deep work of the Spirit happens in the secret place. It cannot be faked or fabricated. We bear fruit; we cannot create it.

- From faith to faith, we seek less of our flesh so that more of His Spirit can flow through us. Could this be spiritual maturity?

- We do not compete with others, but we complete one another.

- If I criticize who I am, I criticize God Himself.

- We shine the light in the darkness and lift them up with affirming words of life, hope and trust.

Chapter 4

- We enjoy the journey because it's part of our destiny, regardless of the destination.

- Constantly knowing that there is more to attain is mandatory for growth.

- Our position in Him determines our provision.

- Some events in our lives are turning points to unexpected outcomes.

- At times, we assume the destination we have reached is final, only to realize it's a page turner to the next chapter in our story.

- Stepping stones pave our walk of faith.

- We put out of our mind our failures and mistakes through forgiveness.

- We cannot follow Him if our eyes are on yesterday.

- It is in the forgetting that we can do the reaching. Both actions are necessary.

- God's way is to use the little that is in our hands and multiply it as we are faithful.

- God sees the end from the beginning and waters our vineyard of today with the harvest of tomorrow in view.

- Not only the steps, but also the stops, are ordered by God.

- When we try to obtain the prize of the high calling of God in Christ Jesus, the decisions we make, and the directions we take, will be heaven bound.

- When we realize the greater glory lies ahead, all the steps in between will be from one level of glory to another.

Chapter 5

- If we count the cost accurately, unexpected trials will be part of expected triumphs.

- The battles we face are not coming in opposition to where we are, but to where we are going.

- satan throws fiery darts aimed at the outward to hinder the inward.

- When we perceive the actual motive behind an action, we no longer waste time fighting what appears to be, but address what truly needs to be overcome.

- Worship takes us into a higher realm where our fighting can be done from above, not beneath.

- In worship, what we have received through the cross is revealed. In prayer, we learn how to use what we have.

- When what we have reasoned, calculated, and concluded has more impact than the Word of God: it must be taken captive.

- We must take authority over the first carnal thought that comes. It is then easier to take captive the carnal thoughts that might follow.

- The moment we step out and become a doer of the Word, opposition increases.

- What came to try to stop us from obeying the Lord is used as a stepping stone to do more in His name.

- When we say yes to the call, we can count on the enemy to fight back. Then our counting is not on the devil's winning, but on our victory. We do not fight for victory, but from a place of victory.

- When we feel the weakest, we are the strongest because we are in Him and He is in us. When we cannot, He can.

Chapter 6

- Fear of the future dissipates when our faith abides in Him.

- The more we feed our faith with the revelation of His love, the more we receive it and are perfected in it.

- It is our growth into the image of Christ, not the growth of a building or a ministry that matters the most.

- We cannot respect what we don't value.

- The restraints and constraints of the Holy Spirit often cannot be understood, only followed.

- What we dwell on, eventually we dwell in.

- We recognize faith vs. fear by detecting flesh vs. Spirit.

- It's never about how great we are, but always how great God is.

- Insignificant encounters can become relevant opportunities.

- When all we see is the Lord, we can walk with His peace guarding our hearts and minds.

- To the degree that we are bound in the Spirit,

we can say no to what is contrary to His purpose and tries to tie us down.

- We recognize our call to action by our inability to get away from it, no matter how much we try.

- He was so bound to the Spirit that bonds and afflictions that tried to deter him could not hold him.

- To be determined is to be fully persuaded.

- Regardless of the directives or circumstances, we can determine to keep on keeping on.

- Unmovable, unbothered, unaffected, unshakable, bound to be determined— we are Ambassadors of Christ.

Chapter 7

- As we are faithful with what He gives us to do, He multiplies it. We must be good stewards of what God gives us, no matter how insignificant it appears to be.

- No assignment appears too small when we serve such a big God!

- When God opens a door of opportunity, we can trust His ability will manifest because of our availability.

- We help Him by not helping Him.

- With every increase comes a new level of authority which is accompanied with a corresponding anointing.

- The Holy Spirit uses us; we do not use Him.

- We are filled to be spilled.

- We do not seek after a title, but after a function. We can trust the unction for the function, not for a title.

- We often only understand our lives by looking backward.

- Our part in co-laboring with Him is to yield and obey.

- Every joint supply, and only God gives the increase.

- Our mouths, hands and feet are His and can only be so when our hearts are His!

Conclusion

- As He has released confirmation, instruction, and revelation to you, remember that He will bestow upon you the anointing for the calling; the unction for every function.

- We can proclaim, "In His hands I rest. In His care I stand. In His Word I abide. In His love I remain. In His glory I glory. In Him I live and move and have my being."

26519461R00107

Made in the USA
Lexington, KY
22 December 2018